Be the best
SWING
on Broadway

By Jennie Ford

Printed by CreateSpace

Available at www.CreateSpace.com/4733539,
Amazon.com, and other retail outlets.

Dedication

To every swing: past, present...and future.

Author's Acknowledgements

Many thanks to all who have helped turn this book into reality. I would like to thank Steve Hanneman, Johnny Stellard, Barb Nelson, Carol McLaren, and Ron Ford, who helped edit it! Thank you to Andrew Ford and Jackie Koehlor for their artistic talents. Kudos to Gemi for introducing me to InDesign. "Merci" to Camille for the endless hours spent entertaining my daughter during the process. A special thanks to Wendi Bergamini, Matt Wall, and Michaeljon Slinger, three of the best people to work with. They allowed me to present their swing methods also. A big shout out to Tara Young and Seth Sklar-Heyn for their input. Much thanks to all those who responded to "what makes a great swing". Thank you to all involved in *Evita*: Rob Ashford, Michael Grandage, Kristen Blodgette, stage management, the cast, the producers, the crew, and the gang at Bespoke Theatricals. I would be amiss not to mention my supportive family from the small town of Humboldt, Saskatchewan, who made me believe I could do anything I wanted with my life!

I have always wanted to give back to the Broadway community that has been so good to me. I love being a mentor and I thrive on seeing performers be the best they can be. It's been a year in the making, but there is finally a "how-to" book for swings! I couldn't be more excited about it!

On January 13th, 2016, Actors' Equity Association declared the first "National Swing Day"!

From this day forward, the 2nd Wednesday of January will be recognized as "National Swing Day".

It's a day to honor the unsung heros of theatre. Look for pictures and stories in the media with **#EquityTeamSwing** and share your own swing stories too!

Table of Contents

Book series

Be the best on Broadway
www.bethebestonbroadway.com

Preface

There are thousands of performing arts schools grooming students for Broadway. Broadway is revered as the pinnacle of every performer's career. It's the "Olympics" of our sport that we have trained and worked so hard for. Would you be confident if you received a Broadway contract that said you were going to be a swing, a dance captain or an understudy? Hopefully you would reply *"yes"*...after all, you have a college degree in the arts, right? These are fundamental jobs in every Broadway musical, so why aren't graduates prepared to do those jobs? The problem is there is "book knowledge" from school and "learned knowledge" from being on the job. This book series bridges the gap between the two.

Students are taught how to pick songs for the roles they are right for, how to perform them, how to study scripts, how to audition and how to show the best of themselves. They study the history of theatre and graduate with confidence that they can nail that audition and land a job. What happens when a talented performer actually books a job? What skill-set do they have to prepare them for the responsibilities that come along with performing under a union contract? It's a rude awakening for some performers to find out about 85% of Broadway performers are *not* principal performers. Even those principals are not always principals! The career choices are endless on Broadway and the idea is to prepare yourself for all opportunities.

"Be the best on Broadway" is a how-to-series that will demystify and teach those who really want a career on Broadway, no matter how much schooling you may (or may not) have. It is the book series of learned knowledge and is intended to be the "go-to" resource for all things Broadway. There is currently nothing like it. Each book is written by a Broadway professional with first-hand experience and is regarded as an expert. Each writer is respected by their peers for the work they contribute on a daily basis on Broadway. The series breaks down the different job particulars in depth and provides tangible Broadway show examples. The goal is to combine valuable insight and resources into one book series to strengthen the chance of success for those who have the Broadway dream!

Buddy, the Worker Bee

    This is Buddy. He is known as the Broadway "worker bee", and he is here to guide you. He will give you some tips, stories, and tricks of the trade, so look for him throughout this book. Buddy knows what it means to work hard and be a part of a team. Broadway is no different!

From the Author

    When I first started in this business, I was a swing and a dance captain on the 1st National Tour of Ragtime. It was an amazing experience but a lot of work. I loved my job, but there was no end to the work I could do to make myself better, the show better, my "Show Bible" better, my note-giving better, and so forth.

    I was nicknamed the "worker bee" by my stage manager and it quickly filtered through the company. Before you knew it, everyone was calling me by that name. I started getting pins of bees, stickers of bees, and many other goodies! This is for all the "worker bees" on Broadway who constantly strive to be the best that we can be.

Jennie Ford

Swing for: *Evita, Hairspray, Urban Cowboy, Ragtime, The Music Man, All Shook Up, Leap of Faith, The Grinch who stole Christmas, and An American in Paris.*

Introduction

This book will prove to be invaluable to swings as well as any performer who wants to learn through this special "lens" ...the eye of a swing! This book looks at Broadway through the unique perspective of a swing. It will help you understand the chorus better and you will gain an appreciation for the old Broadway adage, "the show must go on". Swings are the very reason that the show *can* go on and you will soon see why. It is a job function on Broadway not widely written about or taught in schools. Until now, it's been every actor fending for themselves when they get offered a swing contract. I have been there! It took me many years of being a Broadway swing to figure out what works and what doesn't. I wish I had someone or some book to give me guidance at the beginning of my career.

I think of this book as a "book of secrets" to give you the chance to be an outstanding swing. There is nothing more rewarding than being recognized by your peers for doing your job well. The skills you need go beyond the talent required on Broadway. This book also deals with relationship skills needed for a career on Broadway. "Talent" doesn't give you opportunities, relationships do! There is a high percentage of performers on Broadway who, at one time or another, have been asked to be a swing. The tips in this book will make you stand out as a swing. The goal is not to just do it well, but to become "the best" at it!

This book is geared toward someone with a keen interest in theatre. Beginners may find some of the terms complex at first. The intermediate and advanced actor may know the terminology and are now ready to perfect the skill of swinging. It's a lot of valuable information to take in, so you may not be able to digest everything on the first read-through. The ultimate goal is to have it be the only book you will need to help you be the best swing on Broadway!

Check out these
Broadway stories:

"One night at EVITA, so many guys called out we didn't have enough male swings to cover them all. To fill in the holes, Colin was asked to do a 'chorus adjustment' just for that show and sing one line. He was a great singer and felt very comfortable rehearsing the line 'She really brightened up your out-of-town engagement'. When it came time for him to do it onstage, he had a moment of amnesia because it seemed so foreign to him. Instead, he 'sang-slurred' something like 'She really gave you arms that bound you to the public' (if we had to guess what the words were). It made no sense at all and the whole company had to act like it did and try to move on without laughing. Now imagine what a swing goes through, where everything seems foreign all the time!"
- Jennie Ford

"I love the feeling of being there in support of a swing throughout the show, mostly because when I watch a swing 'do their thing', I question whether I could ever be able to do that. They are so bold and brave and talented!"
- Johnny Stellard

"It was the first time I went on for this particular track in THE MUSIC MAN. In the number 'Trouble', I was supposed to cross downstage and then 2 lines later, the leading character was supposed to cross to me to deliver a line. I didn't cross quite far enough downstage; I was about one foot too far upstage. Rather than cross up to me, the lead chose to sing to an imaginary person, the empty space where I should have been. As swings, we are always prepared to deal with things as they happen. However, often times the 'full time' cast has no idea what to do when faced with something different than what they are used to." - Jeff Williams

CHAPTER 1

What is Chorus work?

To be able to understand what a swing is and does, you have to understand a few fundamentals. All contracts for performers and stage managers on Broadway are administered through Actors' Equity Association. The union mainly uses three categories to distinguish what you do on Broadway: principal, chorus and stage manager. That's it!

The principal contract, also known as a "white" contract, is given to the "leads" in the show. There are many determining factors for how AEA (Actors' Equity Association) decides whether a performer is chorus or principal. A "stand-by" is always on a principal contract. This is a performer who is not in the show every day, but hired specifically to cover a principal role. It's often done to cover the "named star" or the main character(s) of a show. Most stage managers are on a "white" contract.

The chorus contract, known as a "pink" contract, is given to performers in the cast who are not leads. Equity helps categorize every performer's contract by looking at what a performer does for the *majority* of the show. If a performer is working as part of a group for the majority of the show, yet has a solo song to sing or a dance specialty, they are still considered part of the chorus. A chorus actor can be onstage (performing) or offstage (non-performing) during a show. You may also hear the word "ensemble" used for the chorus. That is not an official AEA contract, but it's another word used to refer to the chorus. All swings are on chorus contracts.

By Jackie Koehler

CHAPTER 2

Definition of a SWING

What is a swing? Think of a swing as a "pinch hitter" in baseball, who can substitute for any player on the team. In this case, the "team" is the chorus. A Swing can be hired as a FULL swing, a PARTIAL swing, a VACATION swing or a UNIVERSAL swing.

A FULL swing, most commonly used, is a *non-performing* member of the chorus who learns the tracks of the *performing* members of the chorus. He/she performs when a chorus member is not able to perform his/her own track.

> *A FULL swing in layman's terms:*
>
> *You don't perform every night.*
> *You are expected to be in the building every show.*
> *You get a weekly salary to know a defined number of tracks.*
> *The number of tracks you are responsible for is different in every show.*

A PARTIAL swing is a person in the *performing* chorus who learns the tracks of the other *performing* chorus members for specific "numbers" or scenes. For example: if someone got hurt during a scene, the partial swing (who is already in the show) would be in wig and costume and be able to step into any chorus track quickly for the next number.

A VACATION swing is a person who is hired when an actor is out of the show for any number of reasons (vacation, injury, personal days).

This person is hired on an *"as-needed"* basis. They are not full-time and may be asked to work in different companies of the same show, such as Broadway and/or National Tours.

A UNIVERSAL swing is a person who is hired by a producer when there are multiple companies of the same show. They are hired full time and would go from company to company if the shows were on tour and/or on Broadway. They can be asked to go wherever needed, which could take them out of New York City, the state, or the country.

For example: The Broadway show *EVITA* had:

5 principals onstage
1 principal offstage (which is the "stand-by")
24 onstage chorus (including 2 partial swings)
6 offstage chorus (including 4 full swings and 2 vacation swings)
No universal swings because there was only one company

The 4 FULL swings:

Matt   MJ   Jennie   Wendi

The 2 PARTIAL swings:

Colin   Jessica

The 2 VACATION swings:

Jason   Callie

Here is an example of a typical Broadway show breakdown for principals and chorus (showing who covers whom)

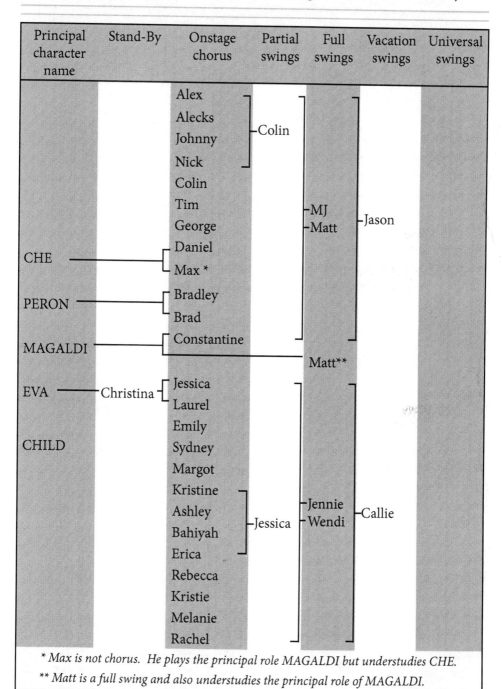

* Max is not chorus. He plays the principal role MAGALDI but understudies CHE.

** Matt is a full swing and also understudies the principal role of MAGALDI.

What does a swing do?

An easier question to answer might be, "What *doesn't* a swing do?".

To an audience, watching the beginning of a musical like *Evita* may look like this: The curtain rises with the actors standing in the dark; they walk downstage while singing; they dance a little and then exit.

To a swing, it looks more like this! At 15 minutes before the show, I have to get my wig on with Wanda, then change in booth #3 with Sam. I have to under-dress for scene 2, then pick up a rosary and candle from the stage-left prop shelf. I stand in the dark, toeing the track, standing stage right of Brad and stage left of Daniel. I sing the alto line, walk downstage and fall to my knees the 5th time I sing "Evita". I wait for "Che" to pick me up off my knees, grab a hanky from him, and wait for Daniel to console me. He leaves me on "Oh, what an exit". I place my right hand on George on "You let down your people". I blow out my candle on the last "Sing you fools" and walk upstage just left of the center speaker. I put my hanky in my right pocket on the last "Sing you fools". I collapse with grief until Alex comes to console me. I hug him at the center speaker with my head downstage of his. I move stage left during the Voleos (dance term) but wait for Sydney to pass so I don't kick her. I exit upstage through catacomb B doing the "trio exit choreography". I take my hat off with Janet at SL5 and go to booth 1 to change. I put props on the shelf in dressing room 3....And this is only the first 10 minutes of the musical!

> *A swing has to have the broadest range of talents in the chorus.*
> *A swing has to have a large vocal range to sing alto to soprano, bass to tenor.*
> *A swing has to be able to dance and partner with anyone in the show.*
> *A swing covers the entire chorus, possibly ranging from a child to a grandmother.*

How do you remember all 50 things? To be an effective swing, you really can't memorize every little detail of every person you cover. You have to have a good system that helps you do your job. That is what this book is for. It will give you all the tools you need to be an effective swing.

The term *swing* and what that job means, is something that is not widely understood. This job position is one of the hardest to cast. A swing quickly becomes one of the most valuable people in the cast because they can do it all.

What is the difference between swings and understudies?

> A swing is a chorus member who covers chorus parts.
> An understudy is a chorus member who covers principal parts.

A swing is a member of the chorus who covers other chorus members. Swings can be onstage (partial swing) or offstage (full swing). An understudy is a member of the chorus who covers a leading role. On rare occasions, a principal actor can also understudy another principal role. A person can be a swing and an understudy at the same time if they cover both chorus and principal parts.

When does a swing perform?

There are many different scenarios and reasons why a swing would perform. With a large cast and a long run, there are going to be shows when one or more cast members have to be out of the show.

- *Vacations*: Actors can take one week's vacation every 6 months.
- *Personal days*: Weddings, graduations, retirements.
- *Bereavement:* Someone in the family passes away.
- *Voice issues:* An actor loses his/her voice.
- *Jury duty:* An actor has to do jury duty.
- *Principal absent:* The understudy covers the principal role and the swing covers the understudy's track in the show.
- *Injuries*: Injuries can happen at the workplace or outside of the workplace.
- *Illness:* There are bound to be illnesses where an actor can't come in or doesn't come in to protect the cast from getting sick.
- *Contractual "outs"*: Some actors may have contract clauses enabling them to film a TV show, record an album, do a concert date and so forth.
- *Swing outs:* Some shows rotate the swings in on a regular basis to keep them practising and help avoid injury to the chorus caused by repetitive movements. There are also instances where the understudies are swung out to watch a show or trail backstage to study the principal part they cover.

Here is an example of a Broadway show calendar. As you can see, the reason someone is out ranges from personal days, vacation, jury duty, being swung out to watch the show and so forth.

Evita
Vacation / Personal Day Summary

MONTH AT A GLANCE
SUBJECT TO CHANGE

As of 1/17/2013

		# SHOWS	OUT	IN	REASON
Week Beginning	06/11/12				
Wednesday-Saturday	6/13-6/16	6	M. Passaro	L. Micklin	Vacation
Saturday eve	06/16/12	1	J. Athens	M. Ulreich	PD
Saturday	06/16/12	2	K. Covillo	J. Ford	PD
Week Beginning	06/18/12				
Monday	06/18/12	1	C. DeCicco	n/a	PD
Monday - Tuesday	6/18-6/19	2	L. Harris	J. Ford	PDs
Wednesday Matinee	06/20/12	1	M. von Essen	M. Wall	Jury Duty (TBD)
Thursday - Friday	6/21 - 6/22	2	A. Pevec	J. Garrett	PDs
Friday - Saturday	6/22 & 6/23	3	GL Andrews	M. Wall	Vacation (contractual)
Monday - Saturday	6/18-6/24	8	M. Passaro	Nolte/Micklin/Ulreich	Vacation (contractual)
Saturday	06/23/12	2	A. Amber	J. Ford	PD
Week Beginning	06/25/12				
Monday-Tuesday	6/25-6/26	2	M. Frank	I. Moner	PD
Monday - Saturday	6/25-7/1	8	K. Covillo	C. Carter	Vacation
Monday - Saturday	6/25-7/1	8	GL Andrews	M. Wall	Vacation (contractual)
Saturday	06/30/12	1	J. Athens	M. Ulreich	PD
Saturday	06/30/12	2	B. Mills	A. Grundy	PD
Saturday Evening	06/30/12		M. Frank's last show/I. Moner's last show		

In the chart above, it lists the cast and stage managers who will be out of the show for different reasons and who will be covering them. If someone only misses a couple of shows, then the company will not hire a vacation swing. In those instances, the full swing will always cover the person who is out of the show. A vacation swing will only be hired if someone is out for a week.

Which swing will be asked to perform?

Let's say Daniel is going on vacation for a week. The company will hire a vacation swing for the week that Daniel is gone.

Daniel
Chorus

Jason
Vacation swing

MJ
Full swing

Matt
Full swing

All three of these swings know Daniel's track so who goes on?

Who goes on?

1) The show may choose to have Jason perform Daniel's track for the entire week and keep MJ and Matt available for other tracks.

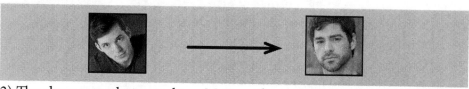

2) The show may choose to have Matt perform Daniel's track for the entire week and keep Jason and MJ available for other tracks.

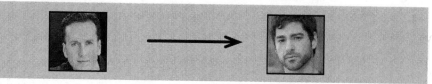

3) The show may choose to have MJ perform Daniel's track for the entire week and keep Jason and Matt available for other tracks.

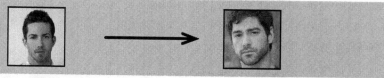

4) The show may choose a combination of swings to cover Daniel, allowing them to cover other people, who may be scheduled to miss that week.

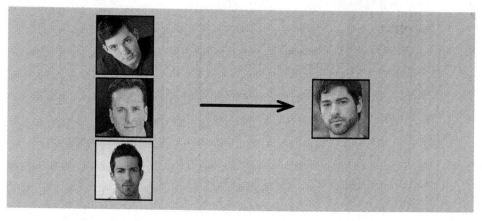

The show decided to put Jason on for Daniel's entire vacation to keep it simple for the wardrobe, hair, and sound departments. There was an older gentlemen who sings bass in the cast, who had 2 personal days that week, so they kept Matt available for that. There was also a dancer with featured partnering, who had 1 personal day, so they kept MJ available for that day.

Relationship between a Swing and a Dance Captain:

A dance captain is hired if there is choreography or musical staging in a show. The dance captain is often one of the swings. If he/she is not a swing, then he/she is in the onstage chorus every show. It's very important to create a great relationship with your dance captain. The dance captain is in charge of knowing where everyone is during the show and can help you answer questions about the tracks you cover. Vice versa, you can also be very helpful to the dance captain with details that you gather about the tracks that you cover. The dance captain is also someone you can go to if there are issues with fellow performers regarding choreography or musical staging. A dance captain is someone you can go to if you have questions about anything. If they don't know the answer, they will find it or point you in the direction of someone who will have the answer.

The dance captain teaches the understudies and swings. When a new show starts rehearsals, it can be difficult for the dance captain to know everything, especially if he or she has their own track onstage, and is not a swing. If he or she does not know something in particular about the tracks you cover, he or she may ask you for the information, if you know it. They will be able to help others with the information you shared with them. At no time, is the swing expected to teach another swing or understudy. That is not in your job description. It is part of the dance captain's job description, and they get paid extra to do so.

What is the difference between a Swing and a Stand-by?

A swing is a chorus member who covers chorus parts.
A stand-by is a principal member who covers a principal part.

Both positions are hired as part of the "offstage cast" for a show. They only perform when someone is out of the show. A swing is hired on a chorus contract and covers multiple chorus tracks. A stand-by is hired on a principal contract and covers one or two principals.

The difference between an understudy and a stand-by is the understudy is on a chorus contract and performs their own track every night. A stand-by is offstage and does not have their own track.

CHAPTER 3

What goes in to Creating a Broadway show

There are many ways a show idea can originate. One example would be where a ***creative team finds a producer***. Perhaps there is a director involved who comes up with a new idea for a show. He or she finds a writer and brainstorms ideas. They come up with a first draft. They then look for a composer and a lyricist to support their ideas. They end up with a full musical score and script. This can take up to a year or two. Then they find a producer or team of producers that are interested in working on that project. The producers get to work raising money and pitching the idea.

Another example is when a ***producer finds a creative team***. Let's say there is a producer who wants to produce a show that has been done before. The producer acquires the rights from the original writers, if they want to use the original music and script. A good example of this is making a movie into a Broadway musical, such as *Rocky* or *Hairspray*. The producer then chooses a director based on who they think is best for this project. The choreographer is also important, so a producer may suggest a choreographer while still giving the director final approval.

It can take years of preparation before a show even begins casting. So congratulations, you finally get the call to do the show! Of all the people who auditioned for the show, you have been hand-picked and you should feel great about it. There are many factors that go into hiring performers. It goes beyond the talent factor, and it's important for an actor to understand both the "show" and the "business" side of theater.

Show business on Broadway

The "**Business**" side

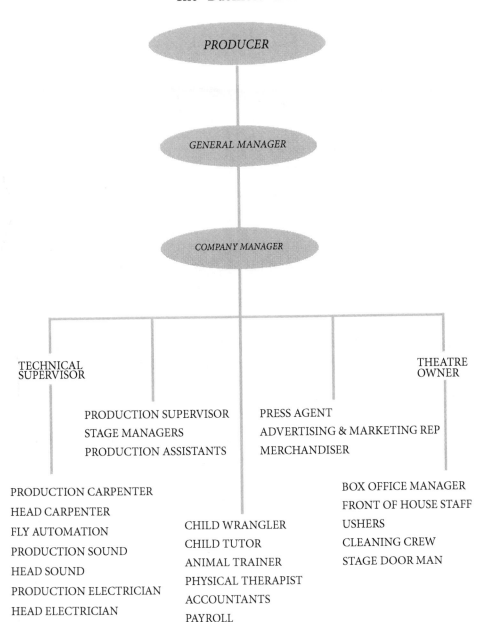

PRODUCER

GENERAL MANAGER

COMPANY MANAGER

TECHNICAL
SUPERVISOR

THEATRE
OWNER

PRODUCTION SUPERVISOR   PRESS AGENT
STAGE MANAGERS   ADVERTISING & MARKETING REP
PRODUCTION ASSISTANTS   MERCHANDISER

PRODUCTION CARPENTER   BOX OFFICE MANAGER
HEAD CARPENTER   FRONT OF HOUSE STAFF
FLY AUTOMATION   CHILD WRANGLER   USHERS
PRODUCTION SOUND   CHILD TUTOR   CLEANING CREW
HEAD SOUND   ANIMAL TRAINER   STAGE DOOR MAN
PRODUCTION ELECTRICIAN   PHYSICAL THERAPIST
HEAD ELECTRICIAN   ACCOUNTANTS
HEAD FOLLOWSPOT   PAYROLL
PRODUCTION PROPS   INSURANCE
HEAD PROPS

Show business on Broadway

The "**Show**" side

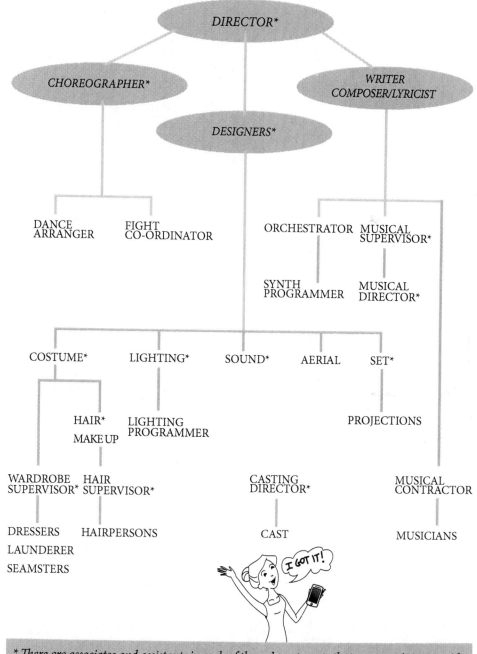

Steps leading up to casting a Broadway show:

Step 1: The director comes up with an overall concept. Then he or she works with the designers for lighting, sound, set, costume, projection and sometimes flying elements to collaborate how best to actuate the concept. Simultaneously, the producers hire a general manager to start estimating the cost of a new production. The producer relies on the general manager to keep track of costs and keep them on budget.

Step 2: The overall ideas are presented to the producer(s). The general manager presents a projected budget based on assumptions and approximations. The budget will assume the weekly operating costs, the ticket sales and the up-front costs. A general manager will assist the producers in controlling costs and track running costs. The producer will go out and get investors for the project to put up money based on how much they think they will need.

Step 3: Once the concept has been agreed upon, the design teams bid out the work to see how much it will cost and start getting "hard numbers" for the budget.

Step 4: Each designer then submits an estimated budget for their contribution to support the director's vision. The lighting designer may say, "With this concept, I can give you this". The costume designer will put together and present his or her "pallet" to the director. The director will look at it and say, "Yes! Yes! But this is too expensive". The director may have to choose where the money is best spent for the overall picture.

Step 5: The producer may be approached with ideas to see if they can increase the budget. For example, they might have a turntable or treadmill or water feature idea to help support the story and help create movement. The producer and general manager will either veto the idea, support it, or try to suggest alterations with regards to the budget.

Determining the cast size.

Step 6: To figure out the cast size, they start looking at "what is on the page". The average musical has 10-12 principals and numerous "specialties" or "bit parts". They will look at the quantity of material each principal does and what is absolutely necessary for casting and which actors could do what. The more principals, the greater the expense because they usually demand a higher salary. Then they figure out the number of chorus needed. Generally, they will need 2 understudies for each principal, even though some understudies can overlap. They look at how many people are needed onstage to tell the story. Also needed are appealing visual stage pictures filling the stage, while vocally pleasing the composer and lyricist. The choreographer will want a certain level of dance expertise to make his or her contribution look impressive. There may be much discussion and compromising to try and please the choreographer, the director and the composer/lyricist. The standard size is about 29 cast members onstage, plus 4-6 swings.

> *The idea of having a "star" or "name" would probably come from a producer, not necessarily the director. The producer may feel it is necessary for ticket sales to have a well-known name in one of the principal roles. This can also affect the budget depending on what the "star" would be able to negotiate in salary, housing, and other perks.*

Step 7: Budgeting for the show. By now each of the design components would have a hard cost estimate. The general manager will figure out what they can afford regarding cast, musicians, wardrobe, and crew. Each theatre comes with it's own "union minimums" that need to be taken into consideration. Some theatres have rules on the number of musicians or crew you must hire, based on the number of seats to sell.

Step 8: Surprisingly, one of the more difficult things to find and negotiate is a theatre rental. There are considerably more shows than theatres available, so theatre landlords can be picky about the shows that come into their theatres. Once the theatre is secured, the general manager and producer will hire a technical contractor or technical supervisor to determine crew costs. They will hire a musical contractor to figure out musician costs. The general manager will start discussions with Actors' Equity Association in regards to actor costs.

Step 9: The general manager will hire an orchestrator and possibly a dance arranger to work on the music before any casting is done.

Step 10: Finally they get to casting.

How does the casting process work?

The composer writes the music with ideas in their head such as, "I imagine 3 violins and 3 voices singing this". The composer will hire a musical director. The musical director will often be the conductor, too. A musical director may help by suggesting voice types to support their vision. There are going to be certain vocal requirements based on the material of the show. The leading roles or principals, as well as their understudies and the rest of the cast, will need to meet certain requirements.

The choreographer will conceptualize each musical number to support the creative team's vision and tell the story. For example: 3 exceptionally strong male/female dancers will be in front, 3 males/females who dance well in the middle and singers who can move to fill in the picture and create the "big picture" effect.

The general manager will hire a casting director. This person helps the creative team break down what they need. The cast is assembled like pieces of a puzzle. The official breakdown that goes out to the public may not be as specific as they internally broke it down to allow for some flexibility in casting.

The internal casting requirements for *EVITA*:

EVA: Strong, versatile, mezzo-soprano. Strong belt. Low E to high G. Must dance well. Charismatic, feminine yet tough. Age range: 15-33 throughout show. Physical and vocal stamina. **(Also need Eva alternate)**
CHE: Rock tenor who sings legit as well. Low B flat to high B flat. Must move well and have physical and vocal stamina.
PERON: Stately, charismatic and charming army officer who becomes President of Argentina. Legit baritone, powerful voice. Low A to high F#.
MAGALDI: Tango singer and Eva's first love interest. High baritone to tenor. Middle C to high G. Also covers CHE.
MISTRESS: An innocent-looking adolescent girl. Must have sweet-sounding high mix. High mix/belt. Low A to high E. Ensemble also.
CHILD (2): Age 9-12. Sweet voice. Middle C to high D. 4 shows a week.

Male Ens 1, 2 & 3: Priority: excellent dancer. Must sing well. 1 Eva's brother.
Male Ens 4: Great dancer/actor. Excellent bass-baritone.
Male Ens 5: Great dancer/actor. Excellent tenor. Does tango.

Male Ens 6: Great dancer. Excellent baritone. Eva's brother.
Male Ens 7: Excellent tenor to cover MAGALDI. Good mover.
Male Ens 8: Excellent counter-tenor to cover CHE. Moves well.
Male Ens 9: Excellent baritone to cover PERON. Moves well.
Male Ens 10: Excellent bari-tenor. Covers PERON and MAGALDI.
Male Ens 11: Excellent bass who moves. Must sing low F.
Male Ens 12: Excellent bass-baritone to play older characters.
Male swing 1: Excellent bass-baritone to cover character roles. Must dance and partner extremely well. Assistant dance captain.
Male swing 2: Excellent dancer and partner. Strong bari-tenor to cover dancer tracks and character roles.
Female Ens 1: (MISTRESS) Alto or mezzo with high belt and nice mix.
Female Ens 2, 3, and 4: Priority is excellent dancer. Must sing well.
Female Ens 5: Excellent dancer. Excellent mezzo sop. Does Tango.
Female Ens 6: Excellent mezzo. Covers MISTRESS. Eva's younger sister.
Female Ens 7: Great dancer/singer to cover EVA. Mezzo sop.
Female Ens 8: Great dancer. Excellent soprano. Eva's sister.
Female Ens 9: Excellent mezzo sop to cover EVA. Dances well.
Female Ens 10: Excellent soprano to strong high D. Moves well.
Female Ens 11: Excellent alto/mezzo. Child's mother vocal solo.
Female Ens 12: Excellent mezzo sop. Moves well. Covers MISTRESS.
Female Ens 13: Excellent soprano to strong, sustained high D. Eva's mother.
Female swing 1: Excellent dancer. Dance captain. Excellent alto/mezzo but can also cover characters and soprano requirements.
Female swing 2: Excellent soprano to high D. Excellent dancer who can partner in tango and money. Covers character roles.

Each track in a show becomes VERY specific. The public breakdown may not be as specific as the internal casting requirements and you may not know all the intricacies when you go into the audition room.

The public breakdown for *EVITA*:

Seeking—Ensemble Singers and Dancers: males and females, early 20s-early 60s, seeking a broad range of ethnicities and excellent singing voices in all ranges, all must understand the Latin temperament even if they don't fit perfectly into the "look," all shapes and sizes to play everything from Generals to peasants, a fully featured versatile ensemble that helps define this world; principal understudies will be assigned from the ensemble. Please prepare 16 bars of a contemporary musical theater song in the style of the show, showing range. Bring sheet music; a piano accompanist will be provided. Bring pix & résumés, stapled together.

A gorgeous-sounding soprano might sing to a high B. She may be asked to vocalize up to a high D. If the actress can only sing to a high C, she may be passed over because the score demands a high D and that one track may be the only one in the chorus singing that note. If a show is already running and they are replacing someone that does an acrobatic aerial to the left, but you only do an aerial to the right, you may be passed over. If a show is already running and they are replacing a girl who is 5'11" and you are 5'2", you may be passed over because they don't want to spend $50,000 to build new costumes. Maybe your voice type fits a track but they are looking for a more classical, rock, folk, soul or country sound. You may be one of the most talented people in the room, but if you don't hit one of the specific requirements, you can easily "fall through the cracks".

To recap, the casting process goes far beyond just talent!

Here's an example of a more specific, public breakdown:

Seeing: ADULTS for the Broadway musical ELF:

FEMALE ENS 1:U/S MISS SHIELDS: Mezzo w/strong belt and legit mix. Must belt to a C and have strong legit F above C. Strong dancer.
FEMALE ENS 2: FEMALE ELF: African American. Strong alto and strong dancer.
FEMALE EN 3: Strong legit soprano who easily sings up high A and strong dancer.
FEMALE ENS 4: U/S MOTHER: Soprano who sings to a high A. Strong dancer.
FEMALE ENS 5: High Soprano who sings up to a high C. Strong dancer.
FEMALE SWING: Must be able to cover all soprano and alto vocal parts. Flexible singer with strong legit voice and belt required. Strong dancer.
MALE ENS 1: Tenor who sings up to a high A. Strong dancer.
MALE ENS 2: Tenor who sings to a high A. Strong dancer.
MALE ENS 3: Santa and Old man U/S: Tenor who sings to high G. Strong dancer.
MALE ENS 4: Tenor who sings up to a high G. Strong dancer.
MALE ENS 5: ELF/WAITER: High baritone who sings to a high F#. Strong dancer.
MALE ENS 6: High baritone who sings to a high F#. Strong dancer.
MALE SWING: Must be able to cover all tenor and baritone parts. Strong dancer.

Once in a while, an actor brings such character to their audition that it outweighs the technical side of the original track. There may be the odd time when you can redefine the predetermined requirements. This usually happens when it's a new show, where they have more leeway. In one instance, a creative team was auditioning for basses and someone, who was not a true bass, knocked their socks off. The director remarked that he was the one who performed from his feet to his head. They looked elsewhere for their bass coverage.

CHAPTER 4

Understanding your Contract

You may or may not have an agent to negotiate your contract. If you do have an agent, they should be familiar with the following terms. However, it should always be your responsibility to critically examine your contract, no matter who negotiates it. Here are some of the more common terms and riders you will see in your contract.

COMPENSATION:

This is the weekly salary the producer will pay you. It will likely include the minimum base salary in the AEA (Actors' Equity Association) Production Contract. It may include a media fee, swing premium, perhaps an understudy premium, and possibly a 6 month rider or term compensation. If you are starting a new show, your compensation may change when Equity does a breakdown of specialty payments. These payments may include extraordinary risk, specialty determinations, and set moves. Once AEA makes the determinations, all actors involved will be paid retroactively from the first public performance. Then the actor will sign a new contract with all the applicable changes to his or her weekly compensation.

HOW MANY TRACKS WILL YOU BE COVERING?

A track is what one actor does for the entire show. If there are 15 actors, then there are 15 different tracks for that show. You will be asked to cover any number of tracks! This is a good question to ask up front to get an idea of how many people you will be required to learn. If you are just contracted as a "swing", they can ask you to cover any of the chorus tracks (dancers, singers, boys, girls). There is a big difference between having to learn 4 tracks versus 28 tracks.

ARE YOUR SWING DUTIES "GENDER-SPECIFIC"?

This is another important aspect to clarify if you can. This will minimize the unexpected surprises, like covering someone of the opposite gender.

AGENCY COMMISSION:

You may chose to authorize the producer to deduct your agent's commission directly out of your weekly paycheck. Currently, the standard applicable commission is 5% during the rehearsal period and 10% during the performance period.

OPENING NIGHT AND PARTY PASSES:

Usually the producer gives 2 opening night tickets. This is assuming the actor will be onstage and not watching the show. If you intend to watch the show opening night, then you better ask for an extra seat with plenty of advance notice or there won't be one left for you. Most producers will not give you an extra ticket in your contract. Instead, they will ask you to notify the company manager separately if you want to sit. Either way, just make sure you have what you need. Producers will often give 3 party passes to each actor for the after-party to celebrate.

PERSONAL DAYS:

You are entitled to take 2 *unpaid* personal days each year of employment for any reason. The reason doesn't need to be disclosed but still needs approval. If you don't have it in your contract, then you are subject to the show's calendar and "blackout dates" where someone has a vacation already scheduled. You can negotiate more days in your contract or be specific about the dates you need to take off. Just know that all this needs to be done in advance and you need to get it in writing!

SWING BILLING:

Some producers bill swings differently than the rest of the chorus. A swing is a function of the chorus, and you can ask to be billed accordingly. The font color would be the same as the rest, but the swings have been boldly italicized, just to clarify the different examples.

1. They may include the swings with the chorus in alphabetical order.

> ASHLEY AMBER GEORGE LEE ANDREWS *WENDI BERGAMINI CALLIE CARTER*
> ERIC L.CHRISTIAN KRISTINE COVILLO COLIN CUNLIFFE MARGOT DE LA BARRE
> BRADLEY DEAN REBECCA EICHENBERGER MELANIE FIELD *JENNIE FORD*
> MAYA JADE FRANK *JASON LEE GARRETT* CONSTANTINE GERMANACOS
> LAUREL HARRIS BAHIYAH HIBAH NICK KENKEL BRAD LITTLE ERICA MANSFIELD
> EMILY MECHLER ISABELLA MONER SYDNEY MORTON JESSICA LEA PATTY
> ALEKS PEVEC KRISTIE DALE SANDERS TIMOTHY SHEW JOHNNY STELLARD
> ALEX MICHAEL STOLL *MICHAELJON SLINGER* DANIEL TORRES *MATT WALL*

2. They may bill the swings at the bottom of the chorus.

> ASHLEY AMBER GEORGE LEE ANDREWS ERIC L.CHRISTIAN KRISTINE COVILLO
> COLIN CUNLIFFE MARGOT DE LA BARRE BRADLEY DEAN REBECCA EICHENBERGER
> MELANIE FIELD MAYA JADE FRANK CONSTANTINE GERMANACOS LAUREL HARRIS
> BAHIYAH HIBAH NICK KENKEL BRAD LITTLE ERICA MANSFIELD EMILY MECHLER
> ISABELLA MONER SYDNEY MORTON JESSICA LEA PATTY ALEKS PEVEC
> KRISTIE DALE SANDERS TIMOTHY SHEW JOHNNY STELLARD ALEX MICHAEL STOLL
> DANIEL TORRES *WENDI BERGAMINI CALLIE CARTER JENNIE FORD*
> *JASON LEE GARRETT MICHAELJON SLINGER MATT WALL*

3. They may list the swings separately at the bottom of the chorus.

> ASHLEY AMBER GEORGE LEE ANDREWS ERIC L.CHRISTIAN KRISTINE COVILLO
> COLIN CUNLIFFE MARGOT DE LA BARRE BRADLEY DEAN REBECCA EICHENBERGER
> MELANIE FIELD MAYA JADE FRANK CONSTANTINE GERMANACOS LAUREL HARRIS
> BAHIYAH HIBAH NICK KENKEL BRAD LITTLE ERICA MANSFIELD EMILY MECHLER
> ISABELLA MONER SYDNEY MORTON JESSICA LEA PATTY ALEKS PEVEC KRISTIE DALE
> SANDERS TIMOTHY SHEW JOHNNY STELLARD ALEX MICHAEL STOLL DANIEL TORRES
>
> *WENDI BERGAMINI CALLIE CARTER JENNIE FORD*
> *JASON LEE GARRETT MICHAELJON SLINGER MATT WALL*

4. They may not include the swings at all on the Title page.

> ASHLEY AMBER GEORGE LEE ANDREWS ERIC L.CHRISTIAN KRISTINE COVILLO
> COLIN CUNLIFFE MARGOT DE LA BARRE BRADLEY DEAN REBECCA EICHENBERGER
> MELANIE FIELD MAYA JADE FRANK CONSTANTINE GERMANACOS LAUREL HARRIS
> BAHIYAH HIBAH NICK KENKEL BRAD LITTLE ERICA MANSFIELD EMILY MECHLER
> ISABELLA MONER SYDNEY MORTON JESSICA LEA PATTY ALEKS PEVEC KRISTIE DALE
> SANDERS TIMOTHY SHEW JOHNNY STELLARD ALEX MICHAEL STOLL DANIEL TORRES

TERM:

A producer may choose to have an actor sign a term contract stipulating a certain amount of time an actor has to stay with the production in exchange for extra payment each week. The term can be something like "6 months from opening" as long as the play remains open. At the end of that term, the producer may elect to ask the actor for another term in exchange for more compensation. The actor has the right to choose it or not. If the actor chooses it, he or she will be paid more but must stay until the date specified. If not, the actor would not receive extra money and would have to give the standard 4 week notice when they want to leave.

FAVORED NATIONS:

This is a rider that is separate from the AEA Production Contract. If there is such a clause, it can be worded many ways. The original intention was that a specific performer would negotiate with the producer that no one else would be getting a better deal than that performer. The favored nation clause can cover many terms, including: salary, housing, transportation, expense money and so on. If there is a favored nations clause for salary, it doesn't mean you can't negotiate in other areas. You can also still negotiate in the "Favored Nation Terms", but it means the producer would have to give the same benefit to everyone who has signed the Favored Nations rider. Just know that it does not guarantee that everyone is making the same dollar-figured salary.

CORPORATE RIDER:

Some actors have their own individual corporations they want to get paid through. This means the only deductions from your paycheck will be union dues. The actor's corporation will be responsible for reporting and paying all taxes and benefits. The producer will still pay the pension and health contributions on behalf of the actor to the Equity League Health and Pension Fund. The producer will also contribute to the actor's 401K plan.

The added benefits of an Equity (union) contract:

In addition to the contract you sign, there are things that your producer is obligated to do under the negotiated AEA Production Contract. Here are some benefits every actor should know about.

HEALTH PAYMENTS:

The producer makes weekly health contributions to the Equity-League Health Trust Fund on your behalf. The amount is calculated by the health fund trustees, consultants and actuaries who are not part of AEA. The fund represents actors, stage managers, and producers; employees *and* employers. Each weekly contribution is credited towards your qualification to receive health benefits. The number of weeks you need to get health insurance can change. Qualifications are set by the trustees of the Health Fund. If you have any questions regarding your health coverage, you should call the health fund at 212-869-9380 or 800-344-5220 (outside NYC only). You can also check out their website at www.equityleague.org.

RETIREMENT PAYMENTS:

The producer pays weekly into the Equity Pension Fund and a 401K plan in your name. You can find out more information on your pension and 401K at www.equityleague.org. You can also call the Equity-League Health and Pension Trust Fund at 212-869-9380 or 800-344-5220 (outside NYC only).

AEA Pension: The producer pays a percentage of your salary (say 6%, but that can change as AEA negotiates the Production Contract) into a pension plan. Pension money will be paid to you when you retire and when you are "vested". Vested means you are fully and unconditionally guaranteed a right to those benefits. The rules to become vested vary for different people and can change. Most commonly, you have to work 10 years under an AEA contract where the producer pays into the pension plan. If you work two weeks or more in any calendar year, that will be credited as 1 year towards the 10 you need to be vested. The current retirement age is 65, enabling you access to those funds.

401K: The producer pays a percentage of your salary into a 401K plan. Currently, it is 3% but can change as AEA negotiates the Production Contract. You, as an employee, also have an opportunity to put away a certain amount of your own weekly salary into your 401K retirement account. This gives you tax-deferred savings on your yearly income tax return. The weekly and annual amounts you can deduct are set by law each year. You will have access to this money when you retire.

VACATION PAY:

You are entitled to a week's *paid* vacation every 6 months. If you do not take a vacation, then the company manager will pay you the money owed. You accrue vacation pay at the rate of 4% of your contractual salary beginning on the first day of employment. If you intend to take a vacation you must give at least 5 weeks written notice. You may not be granted those dates if someone else has a vacation at that time or if management has other reasons for denying your vacation at that time.

WORKERS' COMPENSATION:

The producer pays into a Workers' Compensation Insurance plan. If you get hurt on the job, you are entitled to certain benefits. You can seek medical treatment in regards to the specific work-related injury at no cost to you personally. In more severe cases, the insurance will pay a portion of your salary (not 100%) if you have to miss any work due to your work-related injury. If you get injured at work, report it immediately to your stage manager and fill out the required form. It is called a C-2 in NY.

SUPPLEMENTAL WORKERS' COMPENSATION:

This is something the producer pays into through the Equity-League Health Trust Fund. It is over and above what regular Workers' Compensation covers. This supplemental insurance augments the amount Workers' Comp pays if you have to miss work because of an injury. It would cover more of your lost wages than if you just had workers' compensation. It's important to contact someone at Equity if you believe you may have to miss work due to an injury. Call 212-869-8530 and ask the receptionist to speak with someone in charge of supplemental workers' compensation. That AEA staff person will assist you with the paperwork needed to get the process going.

SICK PAY:

You earn one day of sick pay for every 4 weeks you work. If you are sick on a one-show day, the company will use one of your accrued sick days and you will not be deducted pay for missing the show. However, if you are sick on a two-show day and you have to be out both shows, you will need **2** "sick days". If you don't have enough sick days accrued, then the company manager will just deduct 1/8th of your salary for every additional show missed. If you do not use any of your sick pay, it will be paid out to you. There is a maximum of 11 "sick days" paid out to you for every calendar year. "Sick days" really refer to sick *performances* and not *days*.

COMPELLING CIRCUMSTANCES or EMERGENCY LEAVE:

An actor is entitled to take up to 2 days of *unpaid* leave in each year of employment for a compelling circumstance or emergency. This could be limited to a wedding, graduation, family or medical emergency and must involve an immediate family member.

BEREAVEMENT LEAVE:

Actors are entitled to take up to 3 days of *paid* leave in each employment year to attend the funeral(s) of immediate family members.

DISABILITY LEAVE:

An actor who is unable to work may request an *unpaid* leave of absence for a period of up to 12 months. If granted, you will be able to come back to your position at the end of the leave. This is also used for pregnancy leaves of absence.

There are many other benefits to an Equity contract. The Production Contract is over 150 pages long. Many actors appreciate having a union that protects actors' interests and negotiates fair wages and working conditions. It's a lot easier than one actor trying to negotiate all of these different terms into his or her contract. For more information about the Production Contract, visit www.actorsequity.org. All contract details are listed under the "Document Library". Click the "Agreements" link to take you to the multitude of contracts that Equity negotiates.

"I was swinging 42ND STREET and ended up doing a split-track because one of the understudies was on for Peggy Sawyer. Well, I had forgotten that when an understudy goes on, she does her own track in certain group numbers and I have to do part of Peggy Sawyer's track. So I get on stage, the curtain is about to rise, and the girl I think I'm covering is in my place!!! So literally in 5 seconds, I have to figure out what the Peggy track does, what the hell I'm doing and where I'm going. Luckily I knew the girl I was supposed to end up next to in the number. There was a circle where we had to lay on the floor doing a pattern of opposite choreography in an elevated mirror. She helped me find my spot once I came around the circle (of course, there were two circles going in opposite directions) and as soon as I saw her sit facing one direction, I knew I was supposed to be facing the other direction. It was awful, but I somehow managed to get through. I think I lost 5 pounds that day!"
- Callie Carter

"When I did PROMISES PROMISES, I was under a lot of stress. Not only was it my first time being a replacement in a cast, but it was my first time swinging and also my first Broadway show. I had a put-in for one of the tracks, and was very comfortable in that particular track, but the first time I had to go on in a new track I was terrified. Being an athletic, heavy partnering show we had to do every lift and high risk moment during a condensed 15 minute period prior to curtain. By the time the opening number started, I was already sweating like a pig. I ran to my place where my partner was waiting in a heel stretch, bent over and picked her up. Everything went fine in rehearsal, but now I was drenched and freaking out, and before I knew it, my hands slipped apart and she fell (upside down) on to a desk in front of Sean Hayes. It was like time slowed down- it was only a few seconds but it felt like 30 as I scooped her onto my shoulder and carried her upstage, during which I kept repeating, 'Oh my God. I'm so sorry! Are you okay? Oh my God. I'm so sorry!' I was numb for the rest of the show and I sat and cried in the dressing room as my dance captain rubbed my back telling me that she still trusted me. At the end of the day, she just had a bump on her head and forgave me. I gave her a bottle of 'head-on' as an 'I'm sorry' gift. To this day, I think of that moment every time I partner. It's a constant reminder that I'm not perfect, and that preparation and focus are always necessary. As a swing, mistakes are bound to happen, but we can't let them get us down. We just have to learn from them." - Ian Liberto

CHAPTER 5

Learning People's Names

A significant hurdle you will have to overcome is learning who everyone is, especially those actors you cover. When 100 things come at you from different directions, you will thank yourself for knowing their names when you have to write quickly. It could happen as soon as the first day!

TIP: Get a hold of a cast list, preferably with pictures. Here's how:

1. You can ask your agent to get one before rehearsals start.

2. Ask the company manager or stage manager if they have a cast list.

3. Ask the stage manager at the start of the first day of rehearsal. The "sign-in sheet" is good for this.

4. Do it yourself and look online. There are many resources such as the show's website, playbill.com, and broadwayworld.com.

The pictures on the following page were put together by stage management and given to the cast on the first day of rehearsal. It is referred to as a "Cast Facebook page" and is happening more often. It is used in many departments (wardrobe, sound) so the crew has a good idea of who everybody is in the cast.

Elena Roger
Eva Perón

Ricky Martín
Ché

CAST FACEBOOK
EVITA

Michael Cerveris
Juan Perón

Max von Essen
Magaldi

Christina DeCicco
Eva Alternate

Ashley Amber
Female Ensemble

George Lee Andrews
Male Ensemble

Wendi Bergamini
Swing

Callie Carter
Vacation Swing

Eric L. Christian
Male Ensemble

Kristine Covillo
Female Ensemble

Colin Cunliffe
Male Ensemble

Bradley Dean
Male Ensemble

Margot de La Barre
Female Ensemble

Rebecca Eichenberger
Female Ensemble

Melanie Field
Female Ensemble

Jennie Ford
Swing/Dance Captain

Jason Lee Garrett
Vacation Swing

Constantine Germanacos
Male Ensemble

Laurel Harris
Female Ensemble

Bahiyah Hibah
Female Ensemble

Nick Kenkel
Male Ensemble

Brad Little
Male Ensemble

Erica Mansfield
Female Ensemble

Emily Mechler
Female Ensemble

Sydney Morton
Female Ensemble

CAST FACEBOOK
EVITA

Jessica Lea Patty
Female Ensemble

Aleks Pevec
Male Ensemble

Rachel Potter
Perón's Mistress

Kristie Dale Sanders
Female Ensemble

Timothy Shew
Male Ensemble

Michaeljon Slinger
Swing

Johnny Stellard
Male Ensemble

Alex Michael Stoll
Male Ensemble

Daniel Torres
Male Ensemble

Matt Wall
Swing/Asst. Dance Captain

If you can't acquire their pictures, ask stage management for a blank "sign-in sheet" on your first day. You can then write your own description beside each name to help identify each actor.

EVITA

SIGN IN SHEET

		NAME	FRIDAY	
A.A.	*	A. Amber	ASHLEY	Tall Blond, Vampires, All Shook Up
		G. L. Andrews	GEORGE	Oldest. Phantom 25 YRS.
		W. Bergamini	WENDI	OTHER SWING
		M. Cerveris	MICHAEL	PERON
		E. L. Christian	ERIC	HAIRSPRAY. LEAP.
K.C	*	K. Covillo	KRISTINE	SMASH. TALL. FLEX DANCER.
		J. Cudia	JOHN	
		B. Dean	BRADLEY	DK CURLY HAIR.
		C. DeCicco	CHRISTINA	EVA ALT TALENT HOUSE.
M.D	*	M. de la Barre	MARGOT	New Orleans. Baby girl.
R.E	*	R. Eichenberger	REBECCA	
		J. A. Eyer	AUSTIN	SWING BOOK. TARA
M.F	*	M. Field	MELANIE	SOPRANO. NURSE.
		J. Ford	JENNIE	
		J. L. Garrett	JASON	PITTSBURG
		C. Germanacos	CONSTANTINE	GREEK.
L.H.	*	L. Harris	LAUREL	WICKED Friends
B.H	*	B. Hibah	BAHIYAH	
		N. Kenkel	NICK	
E.M	*	E. Mansfield	ERICA	Blond. Mama Mia
EmM	*	E. Mechler	EMILY	Smiles A lot.
		A. Miles	AVA	
J.P	*	J. L. Patty	JESSICA	
		A. Pevec	ALEKS	Hawaii
R.P	*	R. Potter	RACHEL	Mistress
		E. Roger	ELENA	EVA
G.R	*	G. Ruiz	GABRIELLE	Boyfriend from Canada
K.S.	*	K. D. Sanders	KRISTIE	Blond. Mother of Child.
		T. Shew	TIM	
		M. Simpson-Ernst	MAVIS	
		MJ Slinger	M.J.	Australian.
		J. Stellard	JOHNNY	
		A. M. Stoll	ALEX	
		D. Torres	DANIEL	
		M. Wall	MATT	Dance Cpt Swing
		M. von Essen	MAX	Magaldi.

TIP:
This sign-in sheet had only last names. Write first names to helps you.
Mark asterisks beside the tracks you cover.

Write descriptions on the right to remind you of who people are.
It can be a look, a conversation you had or anything that reminds you of them.

Write short-hand initials on the left to use in notes and charts.
If there are two people with the same initials, add another letter to differentiate the two,
as was the case with Erica and Emily.

If the show is already running, you can acquire a souvenir program or Playbill with the pictures. You can match these with the Cast List names, make notes and put these into your "swing binder".

Ashley Amber | George Lee Andrews | Wendi Bergamini | Eric L. Christian | Kristine Covillo | Colin Cunliffe

Margot de La Barre | Bradley Dean | Rebecca Eichenberger | Melanie Field | Jennie Ford | Maya Jade Frank

Constantine Germanacos | Laurel Harris | Bahiyah Hibah | Nick Kenkel | Brad Little | Erica Mansfield

Emily Mechler | Isabela Moner | Sydney Morton | Jessica Lea Patty | Aleks Pevec | Kristie Dale Sanders

Timothy Shew | Michaeljon Slinger | Johnny Stellard | Alex Michael Stoll | Daniel Torres | Matt Wall

If the show rehearsals haven't started, you can usually find this information online. This information can be found online on sites such as www.playbill.com:

The cast is headed by Grammy winner Ricky Martin (Che), Olivier Award winner Elena Roger (Eva Perón) and Tony Award winner Michael Cerveris (Juan Perón). Christina DeCicco plays Eva at select performances. The cast also features Max von Essen as Magaldi, Rachel Potter as the Mistress, Ashley Amber, George Lee Andrews, Wendi Bergamini, Eric L. Christian, Kristine Covillo, John Cudia, Margot de la Barre, Bradley Dean, Rebecca Eichenberger, J. Austin Eyer, Melanie Field, Jennie Ford, Constantine Germanacos, Laurel Harris, Bahiyah Hibah, Nick Kenkel, Erica Mansfield, Emily Mechler, Ava-Riley Miles, Sydney Morton, Jessica Lea Patty, Aleks Pevec, Kristie Dale Sanders, Timothy Shew, Mavis Simpson-Ernst, Michaeljon Slinger, Johnny Stellard, Alex Michael Stoll, Daniel Torres and Matt Wall.

Once you have this information, you can research online to see faces and pictures. If you will cover all the girls, then research the girls' names for pictures online. If you cover the guys, then research the guys' names for pictures online.

You could make your own "Cast Facebook page" before rehearsals start if you were really keen and wanted to get a good headstart!

"LEAP OF FAITH. There was a lift that was choreographed with a certain hand grip. However, one girl told me not to grab her around the ribs or her rib would pop out. She wanted me to grab her around the waist or under the armpits. Another girl told me to grab her firmly around the ribs. As a swing, you just have to be mindful of the differences in your partners and past injuries that may cause you to alter your partnering from person to person.". - Karl Warden

"I was swinging ELF one year. We had divided up our girls to first and second covers. I had made sure I knew what I was doing on about 4 of them and then got really lazy with my other two. BIG MISTAKE! We had a crazy snow storm that winter and two girls had trouble getting into the city and then could not get parking. So at 15 minutes to places, I had to get ready for one of my second covers who I'd haphazardly watched. Ugh. The first part of the show went fine until we got to the big production number. There was a section where three girls get boxes and then toss those boxes to each other in a circle while standing on set pieces. So everything was going fine until I went to get my box and there was NO box!!! I heard a stage manager yelling my name offstage because that track got her box offstage, but by that time it was too late! I couldn't get the box and get back to my position in time. So I panicked and just ducked behind my set piece. When I looked out, I saw the other swing who was on, trying to figure out if the girl opposite her was going to throw her box. She nodded her head 'yes', the swing threw it but the girl didn't catch it because her hands were full, because she didn't throw her box. And the thrown box hit her in the chest as she dropped the box she was holding." - Callie Carter

"You sometimes have to fill-in for people that are very different than yourself; they are built differently and have different strengths and weaknesses. I went on for a girl who had a very strong core. I had a very weak core but I was very flexible. One dance numbers in MOVIN' OUT was created for this girl I had to cover. I felt that I was poorly suited for the number. I had to do a split in the air with 4 guys holding me and then switch my split to go the other way. Because of my flexibility and lack of core strength, in the middle of switching over, I fell slowly towards the ground as all the men's hands reached to grab me wherever they could and save me. My hands got to the floor and I basically walked all over the place, in a handstand, for '4 -8's' as the guys tried to gather and organize me. The dance supervisor came back laughing saying, 'That went about as long as it could go'. The nice thing about that show was that they didn't care so much about mistakes...as long as you were alive onstage and contributing to the show. The treats of being a swing is being hired to do things you thought you would never do. The challenge of being a swing is that sometimes you are asked to do things that you are not suited for, physically or talent-wise. You are fitting yourself into someone else's skill set and their strengths. It can be a terrific opportunity to grow and be very interesting. Sometimes, you are hired to go on for an ingenue and a character person."
- Lisa Gajda

CHAPTER 6

How to Prioritize

Prioritizing can be most overwhelming when you start as a swing. What do you look at first? There are a couple ways to tackle this question. You should make an *"**Overall** Priority List"* and a *"**Daily** Priority List"*.

An Overall Priority List examines all the tracks you will eventually have to learn and who you could be asked to go on for. A Daily Priority List will help break down your swing duties for the day, and allow you to be prepared for anything that may arise.

When making an Overall Priority List, ask these questions:

1) How many actors in total do I cover?
2) Is there another swing? If so, who will I cover first?
3) Of the people I cover, who are understudies?
4) Are there any personal or contractual days that actors have?

When making a Daily Priority List, ask these questions:

1) What is on the schedule for tomorrow?
2) Does anyone have fittings that will affect me?
3) If so, what will we be doing at that time?

The answers to these questions will help get you prepared.

Making an Overall Priority List:

1. How many actors in total do I cover?

Find out who you will be covering! Make a list of those people. As you read in the previous chapter, you can put an asterisk beside the people you cover on the sign-in sheet you collected. Your contract may not say how many actors or who you cover, so it's best to find out as soon as possible and get acquainted with those particular people.

It may be too early in the process to get the final answer, but someone has an idea of whom you will be covering. Start by asking the stage manager. If he or she doesn't know, they will ask around until they find the answer and get back to you. The stage manager may have to sit down with the other departments (music, dance, direction) in order to figure out which swing would cover what first. It's good to ask the stage manager on the first day so they have a chance to sort things out sooner rather than later. Sometimes, they haven't had the chance to figure the specifics out before the first day of rehearsal. What if someone gets hurt the second week of rehearsals, and no one has figured out which swing goes on first for that track? You may be thrown on for something you weren't prepared for, and that is not a great feeling.

There are some shows where gender does not matter. If a male chorus actor were to call out, a female swing could go on for his track, and vice versa. Check with the stage manager to see if your are expected to know any tracks, or parts of tracks, of the opposite sex. If you are the only female swing or male swing, then you may have to prioritize everyone in the chorus. Start by prioritizing everyone of the same gender as you are.

2. Is there another swing? If so, who do I cover first?

Let's say you find out on the first day that you will be covering 13 girls in total. If there is another female swing, those 13 girls will probably be divided into two priority lists, one for each swing. You will eventually have to know all 13, but in the meantime, you can start focusing on your 6 or 7 actors.

In the case of Evita, Jennie and Wendi were the two female swings. Here is the priority list they were given on the first day of rehearsal after asking the stage manager.

Jennie was given 6 actors		Wendi was given 7 actors	
Ashley	Bahiyah	Kristie Dale	Melanie
Erica	Kristine	Rebecca	Margot
Laurel	Jessica	Sydney	Emily
		Rachel	

From this information, Jennie and Wendi know they have to keep track of where all 13 girls are, but they can focus on the 6 or 7 given in their priority list.

3. Of the people I cover, who are understudies?

This is important to know because, if one of the people you cover is an understudy, it's twice as likely that you could go on for them. If they get sick, you go on. If the lead they understudy gets sick, then they go on for the lead, and you go on for them. Ask the stage manager if there is an understudy list (official or unofficial). Also, ask if there is a priority regarding which understudy goes on first.

TIP:

This is a tricky subject if the show is new because the understudies may not be assigned or enumerated yet. It's best to keep this a quiet conversation between you and the stage manager. Make sure to reiterate you understand the information they give you is confidential and the only reason you want it is to be best prepared for your job.

There are two types of understudy lists: alphabetical and enumerated. If understudies are listed alphabetically, then either understudy can be asked to go on at any time without a preference of who would go first. If it is enumerated, then everyone knows which understudy will go on first.

Here is an example of an Understudy List **alphabetically**:

Understudy List – Alphabetical – as of 4.24.12

Principals	Played By	Understudies
Eva Peron	Elena Roger	Christina DeCicco Laurel Harris Jessica Lea Patty
Che	Ricky Martin	Daniel Torres Max Von Essen
Juan Peron	Michael Cerveris	Bradley Dean Brad Little
Magaldi	Max von Essen	Constantine Germanacos Matt Wall

Here is an example of the same Understudy List **enumerated**:

Understudy List – Enumerated – as of 4.24.12

Principals	Played By	Understudies
Eva Peron	Elena Roger	Christina DeCicco Jessica Lea Patty Laurel Harris
Che	Ricky Martin	Max Von Essen Daniel Torres
Juan Peron	Michael Cerveris	Bradley Dean Brad Little
Magaldi	Max Von Essen	Matt Wall Constantine Germanacos

This is the order in which an understudy would go on. If the first understudy is not available, then the second understudy would be asked to go on. This may happen if someone has it as a clause in his or her contract.

From this list, you can see 2 of Jennie's girls are understudies. However, there is a "stand-by" for EVA who will always go on before the understudies do.

If you also cover the dance captain, you should keep that high on the priority list. You will be swung on if the dance captain is going to "swing out" of the show to watch and take notes.

4. Are there any personal days or contractual days?

Finally, ask the stage manager if there are any contractual personal days coming up for anyone who you cover (or people they cover). This will allow you to determine who you should learn first.

Here is the **Vacation / Personal Day Schedule:**

Evita
Vacation / Personal Day Summary

MONTH AT A GLANCE
SUBJECT TO CHANGE

As of 1/17/2013

		# SHOWS	OUT	IN	REASON
Week Beginning	06/11/12				
Wednesday-Saturday	6/13-6/16	6	M. Passaro	L. Micklin	Vacation
Saturday eve	06/16/12	1	J. Athens	M. Ulreich	PD
Saturday	06/16/12	2	K. Covillo	J. Ford	PD
Week Beginning	06/18/12				
Monday	06/18/12	1	C. DeCicco	n/a	PD
Monday - Tuesday	6/18-6/19	2	L. Harris	J. Ford	PDs
Wednesday Matinee	06/20/12	1	M. von Essen	M. Wall	Jury Duty (TBD)
Thursday - Friday	6/21 - 6/22	2	A. Pevec	J. Garrett	PDs
Friday - Saturday	6/22 & 6/23	3	GL Andrews	M. Wall	Vacation (contractual)
Monday - Saturday	6/18-6/24	8	M. Passaro	Nolte/Micklin/Ulreich	Vacation (contractual)
Saturday	06/23/12	2	A. Amber	J. Ford	PD
Week Beginning	06/25/12				
Monday-Tuesday	6/25-6/26	2	M. Frank	I. Moner	PD
Monday - Saturday	6/25-7/1	8	K. Covillo	C. Carter	Vacation
Monday - Saturday	6/25-7/1	8	GL Andrews	M. Wall	Vacation (contractual)
Saturday	06/30/12	1	J. Athens	M. Ulreich	PD
Saturday	06/30/12	2	B. Mills	A. Grundy	PD
Saturday Evening	06/30/12		M. Frank's last show/I. Moner's last show		
Week Beginning	07/02/12				
Monday - Thursday	7/2 - 7/53	3	R. Martin	M. von Essen (Che) M. Wall (Magaldi)	Vacation (contractual)
Monday - Tuesday	7/2 - 7/3	2	A. Pevec	MJ Slinger	Vacation (contractual)
Monday	07/02/12		Ava DeMary's 1st show		
Monday	07/02/12	1	L. Harris	J. Ford	Vacation
Tuesday	07/03/12	1	E. Mansfield	J. Ford	PD
Tuesday	07/03/12		Mavis Simpson-Ernst's 1st show		
Tuesday - Sunday	7/3 - 7/8	7	L. Harris	C. Carter	Vacation
Thursday - Saturday	7/5-7/7	4	A. Pevec	J. Garrett	Vacation

Helpful information about the people Jennie covers:

1. Kristine Covillo does not cover anyone, but she has a contractual personal day in 2 weeks.
2. Christina DeCicco, Eva's stand by, is gone for a day and so is one of the understudies. Jessica is the only Eva understudy in the building for that day.
3. Laurel Harris has personal days the week after Kristine.
4. Ashley Amber has personal days after that, and she also has a featured dance with the lead.

You should consider the dates of personal days, known injuries, illness going around the company, dance captains, understudies, reputation for calling out or never being out and absences for fittings.

Now you can complete your Overall Priority List:

Jennie was given 6 girls to look at first. She looked at all the vacations, personal days, understudy information and reputation in order to make her priority list. The following would be a good start to her priority list and here are the reasons why:

1. KRISTINE COVILLO: She has the first personal day of all the girls she covers. She wants to be really prepared when she go on and this could be the first time she goes on. She wants the company to respect the work she is doing, and her efforts will be shown the first time she go on. It's a guaranteed performance, whereas some of the others are speculative.

2. LAUREL HARRIS: She will look at her, too, because she has personal days shortly after Kristine, and she won't be able to watch her while she is on for Kristine.

3. JESSICA LEA PATTY: She understudies someone, so there is twice the chance that Jennie could go on for her track. She is also the only understudy for Eva in the building on one day.

4. ASHLEY AMBER: She has personal days and dances a feature with the lead.

5. ERICA MANSFIELD: She has a difficult track and more risk involved in her show than some of the other dancer/singers.

6. BAHIYAH HIBAH: She has an equally difficult dance track, but seems really physically fit and stable and not likely to call out of her show.

You can't learn everyone's track at once. This will make you feel overwhelmed. If you try to do this, you may fall prey to learning "a little of everything, master of none". Your goal is to be really good at all of the tracks so you feel satisfied when you go on. Start by getting a few tracks solidly under your belt and then it will be easier to learn more. BUT.... it's a good idea to learn everyone in broad strokes while you concentrate on your priority list. This means that if you have to make a choice of who to watch at any particular moment, pick the one that is a priority. If you are in rehearsal and learning general choreography for the last 3 people on your priority list, learn them anyway because you never know what can happen. Now that you are learning people's names and know who you are going to start focusing on, you are ready to rock n' roll!

Making a Daily Priority List:

In addition to your Overall Priority list, you will need to make a Daily Priority list. As you go through rehearsals and tech, actors will constantly be pulled away for fittings, and you will have to step in. This is in front of the entire cast and creative team, so you want to be prepared.

Start by taking a look at the next day's rehearsal schedule:

EVITA - DAILY REHEARSAL SCHEDULE - SUBJECT TO CHANGE
Tuesday, January 24, 2012   Rehearsal #2

TIME	ROOM 6A	ROOM 6B	ROOM 6C
9am-10am	Pre-Production/Set up	Pre-Production/Set up	Pre-Production/Set up
10am-1pm	MUSIC w/Waldrop FULL ENSEMBLE - Learn and Review * Principals join as available from other rehearsals.	Pre-Production w/Ashford	10-11:30 MUSIC w/Blodgette and Grandage R.Martin
			11:30-12:30 SCENE WORK w/M. Grandage E.Roger, R.Martin, C.DeCicco
			12:30-1:30 MUSIC w/Blodgette and Grandage M. Von Essen
1:30-2:30pm	LUNCH	LUNCH	LUNCH
2:30-6:00pm	DANCE w/Ashford FULL ENSEMBLE - Buenos Aires *Principals joins as available from other rehearsals ADD: C.DeCicco 3:00pm ADD: E.Roger at 3:30pm		2:30-3:30 MUSIC w/Blodgette and Grandage On This Night.... R.Martin, E.Roger, M.VonEssen
			3:45-5:30 MUSIC w/Blodgette and Grandage M.Cerveris

FITTINGS
11:00am   J.Ford at New 42 Studio - wig wrap
11:30-12:30pm   M.Cerveris at New 42 Studio - wig fitting
12:30-1:30pm   E.Roger at New 42 Studio - wig fitting
6:00-6:30pm   M.Field at Costume Studio (555 8th ave) - wig wrap
6:00 - 7:30pm   L.Harris at Costume Studio (555 8th ave) - fitting

Who has fittings tomorrow?

When is it? What will we be doing?

The daily schedule will have fittings listed and will give you a "heads up" as to whom you should be focusing on. It will also tell you what production numbers you will be learning or rehearsing during that time. You can get a better idea of what to be prepared for so you feel confident and make a good impression.

TIP:

Learn first and last names! Scheduling is often done with last names. If you aren't aware of who the people are that are scheduled for fittings, you may miss something that involves you.

So taking a look at tomorrow's fittings, what can we find out to help us?

FITTINGS

11:00am	J.Ford at New 42 Studio - wig wrap
11:30-12:30pm	M.Cerveris at New 42 Studio - wig fitting
12:30-1:30pm	E.Roger at New 42 Studio - wig fitting
6:00-6:30pm	M.Field at Costume Studio (555 8th ave) - wig wrap
6:00 - 7:30pm	L.Harris at Costume Studio (555 8th ave) - costume fitting

You can use the daily schedule to help plan your day. Look at the "FITTINGS" at the bottom, then use the schedule as a guide to see when you will need to step in and what you will need to be prepared for.

- Jennie (J.Ford) is the swing, so she would have to see what music she missed learning in rehearsal.
- Michael (M.Cerveris) and Elena (E.Roger) are principals and they are not scheduled for rehearsal during their fittings. So, no understudy or swing has to worry about it.
- Christina (C.DeCicco) is a stand-by and is not scheduled for rehearsal during her fitting. So, no understudy or swing has to worry about it.
- Melanie (M.Field) and Laurel (L.Harris) will have to leave early for their wig fittings. Wendi and Jennie will have to keep track of them during the afternoon dance rehearsal of "*Beunos Aires*", so they can step in the last 15 minutes. The choreographer may want to run the whole number before the end of the day.

CHAPTER 7

Learning Music, Choreography and Staging

Learning music, choreography and staging is somewhat of a personal process. It's dictated by your learning style. One person may work well with pictures and visualization while others may do better with words. Some people may just need to do it over and over again, strengthening muscle memory. One actor may read music, while the other actor does not. This chapter gives you some ideas as to how you can approach it.

The learning process is slightly different, depending on whether you are hired for a new show or an existing show. If you are hired for a new show, you will be learning the show with the rest of the cast. It sometimes can be a more difficult process. Everything is constantly changing, versus being hired for an existing show, where they already know exactly what everyone does.

If you are hired for an existing show, you will be learning without the rest of the cast. You will be given a lot of "specifics" that have already been ironed out in the past rehearsal process. If you are learning music, it will likely be you and the musical director in a room by yourselves. If you are learning choreography, it will likely be the dance captain (or resident choreographer, dance supervisor) and you in a rehearsal studio or on the stage. If you are learning staging, then the stage manager (or resident director) will work with you in a studio or on the stage to teach you the direction.

Learning Music

When learning music, bring a pencil, an eraser, and a recording device. There will be rows of chairs with music stands in front of each chair. If you haven't already been given a score, then one will be placed at each spot. If they don't have assigned names, then just claim one.

The musical director will most likely want everyone to sit in vocal sections according to your vocal range (bass, baritone, tenor, alto, soprano). They usually know what to expect of you from your audition and they have hired accordingly to cover the score.

Ask the musical director if he/she wants you to learn all vocal parts or just concentrate on one first. If you are told to learn one part, then sit with that voice group. If you are asked to learn all, then sit between the voice groups so you can sing along with each group when they learn it.

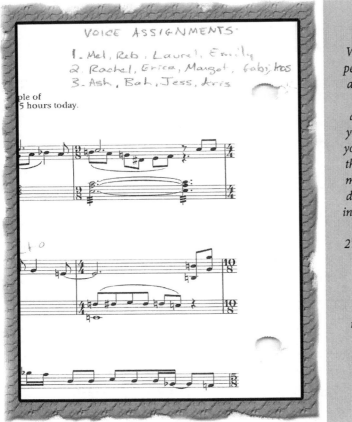

TIP:

Write down the people you cover and what voice type they are assigned to, so you can remind yourself later. In this instance the musical director divided the girls into three groups:
1's (top),
2's (middle), and
3's (bottom).

It's one more thing that will make you look prepared.

You can write it right in your score.

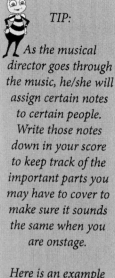

TIP:

As the musical director goes through the music, he/she will assign certain notes to certain people. Write those notes down in your score to keep track of the important parts you may have to cover to make sure it sounds the same when you are onstage.

Here is an example where there are only 2 people on each of the top three notes of the chord, so it's important you know who sings what, and when.

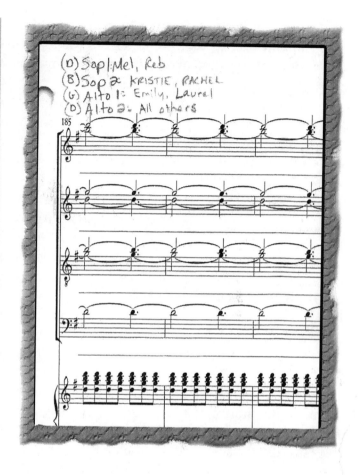

As the vocal groups learn their music, record the notes and sing along to get it in your voice. Don't be shy! It makes a musical director more confident in the swings to see they are learning their music and singing confidently.

There will be solos assigned as everyone learns the music. Notate who those people are, so you remember when you review your music. Pay particular attention if you cover someone who has been assigned a solo, such as: one part of a vocal trio, the "riff" section in a song, or a particular solo line.

Sometimes the musical director will want to hear a few parts together to see if they have the right mix. You may want to ask the musical director if they would like you to sit out so they can hear the onstage blend. There is a fine line between asking too many questions and being annoying versus helpful. Take the "temperature" of the room to see if it's an appropriate time to ask the question. If you feel it may not be the best time, wait for the next break and approach the musical director privately.

It is helpful to go over the music you have learned at the end of each day. Play it in your car, on the train, or at home before bed. The more you learn as you go along, the more it will help you in the end. You want the music and the lyrics to feel second nature. It will help you when you learn choreography or staging later on.

Learning Choreography

When learning choreography, take comfortable clothes and shoes to dance in. You should also take a pencil, eraser and some paper to write on. The paper depends on your personal preference: loose leaf, blank, lined, coiled notebook, binder. A clipboard can come in handy when you need to walk around the room and jot things down.

If the choreographer starts by teaching general dance terminology on "its feet", then grab an area of the dance floor and learn along with the rest of the chorus. If it looks like the choreographer will be spacing the number while teaching the choreography, then it's best to grab an area towards the back, sides, or front of the room, off the dance floor. The choreographer can then look at the overall spacing with the onstage chorus.

If there is partnering involved, grab the swing of the opposite gender to practice. If there is no one to practice with, just mark the partnering section as best you can. This will help yyour body's muscle memory. Then try to involve a partner (dance captain or chorus member) at a break, or later date, to try out the moves.

Don't worry about writing the choreography down immediately as you are learning it. It's best to get it into your body first. You can write it down on a break or after you learn it that day. You will need to refer to it later. Not even Superman would be able to remember the little choreography nuances that you will learn. By the time you have learned many people's choreography and nuances, you will be glad you wrote the details down.

There are many ways to help remember:

1. Write the choreography in your score next to the corresponding music.
2. Write the choreography on a blank piece of paper.
3. Tape yourself doing the choreography.

Here's an example of writing the choreography in your score.

Here's an example of writing the choreography on a blank piece of paper.

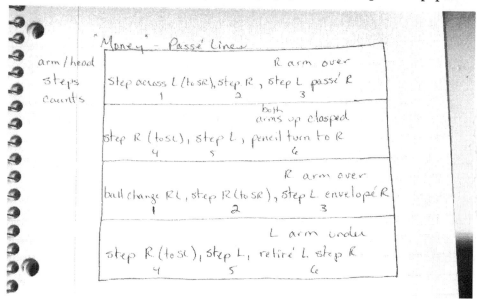

When writing down choreography, there are a number of components that you can include to be effective, helping yourself later.

You should include:
1. What is happening with the head and arms.
2. The particular actions of the body (particularly the feet).
3. The counts or timing of the dance steps.

TIP:

Stick-figure drawings are useful to help you remember.
They are most helpful when actors are given specific poses by the
choreographer needed when you go on for their track.

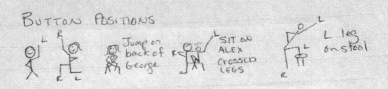

TIP:

You can also come up with your own short hand notation to help you write down
choreography. In the example below, the swing chose to use a triangle symbol for
every "ball change" instead of writing the word out each time.
The "x" was used every time you were to cross one foot over the other.

$\triangle$LR   = Ball change LR.

XLR   = Cross L foot over R and step R.

TIP:

Avoid the possibility of insulting a choreographer by dancing someone else's
choreography in front of him/her. I saw a dancer practising choreography
from another show during a rehearsal break. The cast was enjoying it but our
choreographer was very offended and reprimanded him. You never know what pressure
and stress the choreographer is going through.

Learning Staging

Staging is different from choreography. Choreography is the movement you learn. Staging is where you are placed on the stage while you are doing the choreography. To keep track of where the actors are on stage, you need a system to record those details. This will be a personal preference. This chapter will give you some suggestions.

There will likely be some forms of measurement used when staging each number. Some shows will have numbers at the front of the stage. This helps position the actors "**width-wise**" from left to right on the entire stage. When using numbers, the center mark is zero and the measurement gets bigger on each side; stage left and stage right. You may be told, "move stage right to 5" or, "put your left foot on stage left 12". That would mean move 5 feet stage right of center or 12 feet stage left of center.

Some shows choose to have colored lights across the front instead of numbers. You may be told, "go between the blue and yellow" or "stand on green". It can get very specific, especially when you are working with large casts and creating detailed, balanced pictures with the choreographer.

Most importantly, the stage is two dimensional. The choreographer and director may also tell actors where to be "**depth-wise**". They may use the wings, marks on the stage or "track lines" where the automation will run. This helps placing the actors depth-wise from upstage to downstage. For accuracy, you have to mark where the actors are, both left to right and upstage to downstage. You may have to walk around the room while actors are being positioned, so you can see exactly where they are placed in relationship to other actors.

TIP: What do you do if there are no numbers?
Take a look at the stage and write down any markings that are consistent throughout the number that can be used as reference (such as tracks, wings, speakers, set pieces, platforms).

Here are four different ways to keep track:

1. Write *many* stage positions on one page.
2. Write *one* stage position per page using the production stage charts.
3. Write *one* stage position per page using blank paper.
4. Input everything into Stage Write, the ipad app.

1. Write many stage positions on one page:

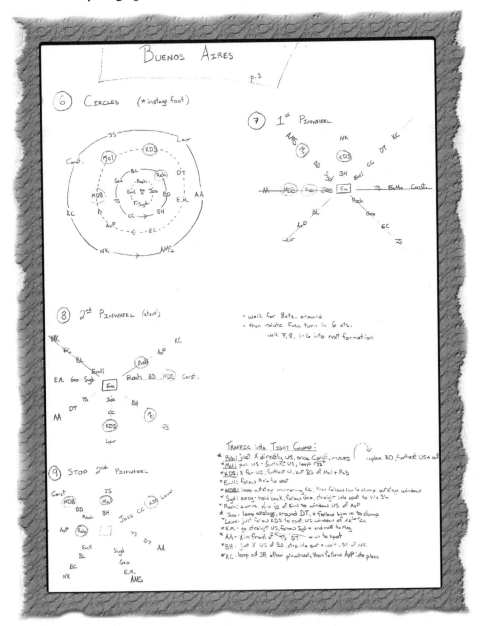

The strength of this system is that it is easy to look at all the diagrams quickly with lots of information on one page. The downside is you would have to write in all the information, such as numbers and tracks and such. You can leave information out to keep it looking cleaner, but your note-taking will be less specific.

You can write notes on the side to remind yourself of the details of each picture. Details would include director/choreographer notes or intentions. It could include traffic into or out of the formation, prop information, timing or counts that you must remember and so on.

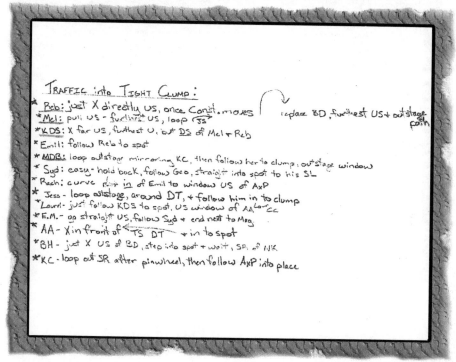

It is good to place your papers on a clipboard and have a pencil and eraser close by so you have the freedom to walk around the room while jotting down spacing. (Attach the pencil to the clipboard with velcro or magnetized tape). You may also have to mark in some set pieces on your chart.

2. Write one stage position per page using the production stage charts:

You can ask stage management if they have any blank production stage charts. It is commonly called a "chart"; there are different ones for every scene. They can be photocopied to any size, but you would probably start with a regular sized piece of 8 1/2 x 11" piece of paper.

If there are no charts, then the stage manager may ask the set designer for a template. A production assistant (PA) may be asked to make copies. It's not part of their job, so be gracious and very appreciative.

Here is an example of a **blank chart**.

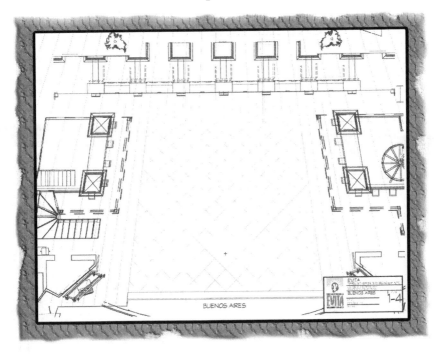

Here's an example of the **chart filled in with names**.

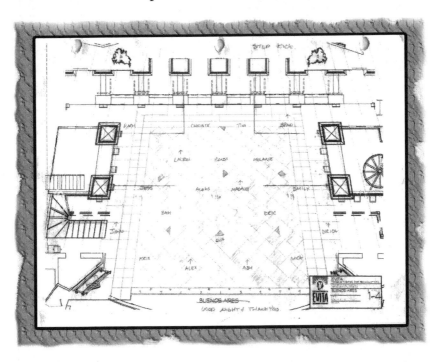

As the director or choreographer is placing the actors, write down their location on the chart. You will have a new chart for every major position change throughout the number. It is helpful to title each chart using lyrics, dialogue, or specific references (such as "the clump" or "the mountain"). You will have numerous charts for one number. That's why it's important to keep your system labeled and organized.

Instead of writing people's names on the chart, you can create a shorthand for identifying who they are. You could use their initials or character names. If you don't know their last names, then write their full first names or whatever you can to get started. Using character names is always helpful, especially when an actor is replaced by another. You won't have to change the names in your charts.

Here's an example of the **chart filled in with initials** instead of names.

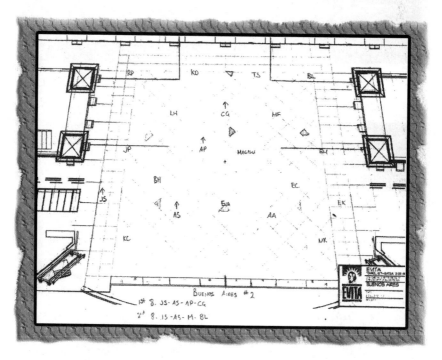

Ultimately your first pass will be "draft charts", and you can perfect your system later. It will go quickly, and it will be messy. The most important thing is to write down *everything* you can. There will be many changes, so write in pencil!

3. Write one stage position per page using blank paper:

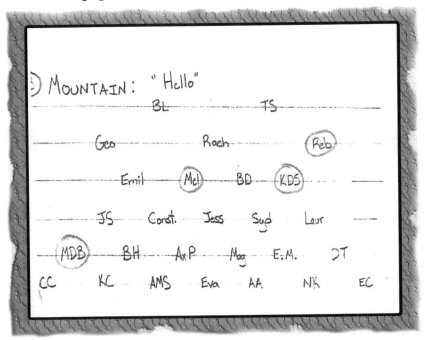

In this instance, the swing places the positions on a blank piece of paper. Lines are drawn to show the actors who should be in the same line. There is a title showing what position it relates to in the music. The swing circles the tracks she covers. The only things missing are the numbers but the position is very clear and easy to read.

4. Stage Write application:

There is a great new application for the ipad called Stage Write. It allows you to upload blank stage charts (pdf's) to create your book. It has many great, helpful features. The pros of this program are that it doesn't waste paper, you can save many versions, you can switch between audience and performer point of views and it's easy to email or print. If the stage manager calls to tell you you're on, you are more likely to have your ipad with you rather than bulky swing books. The cons are that it relies on battery power and you always want the information accessible. It takes a while to become quick at using the program. Currently, there is no easy way to separate out the specific people you cover. To learn more about this app, visit www.stagewritesoftware.com or check out many tutorials about this program on You Tube.

Here is an example of a **chart, in the Stage Write app**.

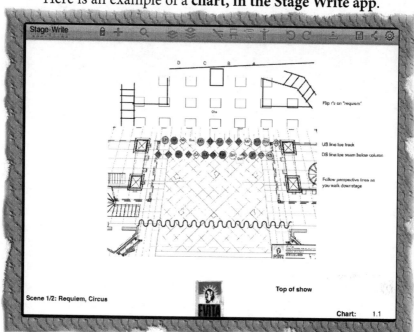

Do you prefer the Audience or Actor's point of view?

Here's an example of an alternate version, from an actor's point of view.

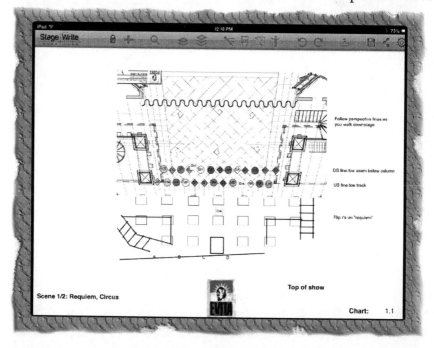

Write everything down

This is what will make you stand out in the long run. You can't possibly keep all the little things in your head, so write everything down. Not only will it be useful later, but it will give you "street credibility" when you are able to state what the director's intentions were a month from now. The rest of the cast is on their feet and do not have the luxury of carrying a pencil and paper. They may forget the details down the road. You have an advantage here so make the most out of it!

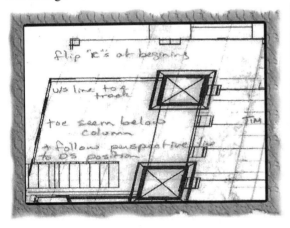

Write everything you hear in the corner of your chart that pertains to that number.

The musical director asked everyone to flip their "R's" singing Requiem.

The choreographer placed the two lines specifically for lighting (toe track and toe seam below column).

The director wanted the actors to walk downstage following the perspective lines on the stage vs walking straight downstage.

When writing the information down for the first time, you can sit somewhere or walk around as the company is being placed. If you sit, you can be at the swing table or at your own space you have created somewhere in the rehearsal room. If you walk around, it's best to have a clipboard to put your papers on so you have a "mobile table" to write on.

CHAPTER 8

Contact, Pre-Rehearsals

If you are hired for a new show, you may receive many emails and phone calls from various departments involved in the show even before you meet anyone. The costume department, in particular, likes to get working on things as soon as possible because it takes a long time for custom clothes, shoes and wigs to be made.

Here are some examples of what you can expect:

- Your company manager may welcome you and relay any messages from departments involved with the show.
- The costume department will likely ask to get your body measured at the costume shop for the show.
- The costume department may ask to get your feet measured at a shop or multiple shops that will be making the shoes.
- You may be asked to get your head measured for wigs. A wig measurement will entail putting your hair in a wig prep. Your head will be wrapped in plastic wrap and clear tape so they can measure and mark your hairline.
- The press department may contact you regarding a "bio" (biography) and headshot for the program.
- You will hear from your stage manager as the rehearsal date nears.

If you are rehearsing for an existing show, you are likely to hear from only the stage manager and/or company manager about your rehearsal specifics.

Here's an example from the hair department regarding wigs and facial hair.

Dear EVITA Cast Member,

I hope this email finds you well. Our wig and hair designer will be in town from London in a few weeks and would very much like to meet with each of you individually for fittings. Would you please email back and let me know your availability on Monday 10/17, Tuesday 10/18 and Wednesday 10/19.

Richard will need approximately 45 minutes – 1 hour with each of the women and approximately 15 – 30 minutes with the men. Men, if you can please avoid using any gel or hair product prior to your fitting.

Please feel free to call me with any questions.

Here's an example from the wardrobe department regarding costume measurements and fittings.

Hello,

This is your Costume Design Associate and Costume Design Assistant working with Christopher Oram on the costume design team for the upcoming Broadway production of Evita. Congratulations on being cast in this exciting revival! We are starting to put things together in our newly set up design studio, and we need to schedule a time for you to stop by to be measured for your costumes and shoes.

The studio is located at 555 8th Ave. We will be in Mon. Aug. 29th thru Fri. Sept. 2 or Tues. Sept. 6 thru Fri. Sept. 9.
Please contact Christina by e-mail or phone to set up a measurement appointment.

We look forward to meeting you and working with you soon!
Best, Costume Design Associate & Assistant Evita Broadway

Here's an example from the press department regarding headshot and bio.

Hello:

We in the Press Department are currently putting together the program. The program has an early deadline so we are collecting bios and headshots prior to the first rehearsal, and we need a few things from you:

Bio of 40 words.
Headshot, specs should be 300 dpi
We would like to verify the correct spelling of your name.

We need these by next Friday, December 30th. Please call if you have questions.

Here's an example from the stage manager regarding the first day of rehearsal.

> *Company,*
>
> *This will confirm the details for the first day of rehearsals for EVITA on Monday January 23rd. Location: New 42nd Street Studios (229 West 42nd Street) On the first day, you will be required to check-in at the lobby desk where you will receive an access pass. After the first day, you simply show the access pass to security and they will let you into the building.*
>
> *Schedule for 1st day: (subject to change)*
> *10:00am: Actors Equity Meeting – Full Cast Called – room 6B*
> *11:15am: Meet and Greet with full production team – room 6A*
> *Cast, creative team, producers, designers, management, staff. Food will be provided*
> *12:15pm: Rehearsals – Specific schedule to be determined*
> *Be prepared to sing and dance*
> *1:30pm-2:30pm: Lunch*
> *2:30pm: Continue Rehearsals*
> *6:00pm: End of Day*
>
> *General Schedule while at New 42: Rehearsals are scheduled at 10:00am and will go until 6:00pm or 6:30pm, Monday-Saturday. Lunch will be from 1:30p-2:30p or 3:00p (The span of day and length of lunch is determined by a company vote on the first day of rehearsal). Sunday will be our day off while in the rehearsal room. The rehearsal rooms open at 9:00am on a daily basis for those who would like to warm-up prior to 10:00am.*
>
> *Schedules, call-times, and fittings will be emailed to everyone on a daily basis each evening for the following day's rehearsal. All scheduling is communicated by e-mail. Please remember that all schedules are subject to change at a moment's notice and that you should be prepared to rehearse all of the allowable hours every day. A general production calendar will be distributed on the first day of rehearsal to give you an idea of technical rehearsals onstage, previews, etc.*
>
> *Things To Bring: Scores will be provided to everyone on the first day. Please bring a recording device to record your vocal parts. Everyone should be prepared to dance so please bring appropriate clothing. Men should bring dance and/or character shoes. Women should bring a dance shoe with a heel.*
>
> *Lockers will be provided in the studio dressing rooms so you can keep your things overnight. The lockers are equipped with individual combination locks so you do not need to bring your own. The studios are equipped with a green room, lunch area, refrigerator, and microwave on the 5th floor for those who want to bring their lunch. Food is not allowed in any of the studios, only in the green room.*
>
> *If you have any other questions prior to the 23rd, please feel free to contact me via this e-mail address or on my cell phone. We look forward to seeing you then.*

"One of the more challenging things swings sometimes have to deal with is having an actor come to them to say they may not make it through the show and to get ready. A 'heads up' is always appreciated but the correct protocol is to tell the stage managers. Then they give official notice to the swing that he/she will go on. In one of my shows, the women wore extensive make up and it took a long time just to do the make up. It wasn't something you could quickly go on for and you didn't want to get into make up if you didn't have to. One girl told me she may not make it through the show. The stage manager told me to get ready. I did the make up and wig prep all to be told at intermission that the girl was going to push through and finish the show. Ugh! After all that prepping, I was just ready to go on! I wished the actor would have rested and just taken care of herself. It's hardest when it is not a clear decision. Sometimes it's better if a decision is made and the swing, along with all the departments can plan accordingly."
- Anonymous

"I was on for a girl in EVITA. There were 8 maids who did a costume change onstage for Eva Peron while she sang. I was covering the girl who took off Eva's robe, held out Eva's blouse for her to slip into, and then buttoned and hooked Eva's skirt. All the maids worked together. Everything was going well until I realized the blouse was inside out! Eva was singing and had already put her arms through and the maid in front was trying to button it. There was no time to change it. Luckily the maid in front just calmly buttoned it inside out to save my butt. Eva had to rip the blouse off in another quick-change onstage and I was paranoid it would cause her trouble. Later, she said she noticed it was a little harder to undo, but didn't even notice that it was inside out. From then on, I always checked (and rechecked) the clothing presets."
- Jennie Ford

CHAPTER 9

What to expect the First Day

What happens on your first day of rehearsal? It depends on whether you are hired to start a new show with everyone else or if you are going to replace someone in an existing show.

First day of rehearsal for a New Show

If you are starting a new show, you will be "hitting the ground running". There are so many things that everyone has to learn. As a swing, you will be learning more than anyone and faster than anyone. There are many tips to keep you on top of your game. These tips will help you stand out as an extraordinary swing and have the company singing your praises.

First day of rehearsal for an Existing Show

If you are the only person being hired to learn an existing show, then you will spend much time learning one-on-one. You will not be learning with the full cast. If you are rehearsing at the theatre, then look for the sign-in sheet, as they may put one up for you. If not, then don't worry about signing in. The stage manager will see you are there at the start of your rehearsal. This chapter will primarily address what to expect with a new show. The learning curve is similar, but more difficult.

Signing In

When you get to the place of rehearsal...sign in! Look for the call board and the sign-in sheet. You will have to initial beside your name to let stage management know you are in the building. You will be required to do this in the morning and again after lunch (after every time you leave the building and come back). Get in the habit of doing this so stage management doesn't have to look for you.

Callboard   Sign-in sheet

Daily Rehearsal Schedule

After you sign in, look for the daily rehearsal schedule, which will be on the callboard as well. It will tell you how the day will be run. You will see if you may stay in your street clothes or if you will be required to change into dance clothes and warm up if there will be dancing taught. It's a good idea to be prepared to dance or sing on the first day because the schedule it always subject to change!

Pay attention to the fittings to see if anyone you cover will be missing during the day, and when. This is the reason you need to find out who you cover as soon as possible. You may be thrown in the first day. It may be helpful to refer back to Chapter 6, regarding daily priority lists.

Here is an example of the **First Day Rehearsal Schedule**:

EVITA - DAILY REHEARSAL SCHEDULE - <u>SUBJECT TO CHANGE</u>

Monday, January 23, 2012   Rehearsal #1

TIME	ROOM 6A	ROOM 6B	ROOM 6C
9am-10am	Pre-Production/Set up	Pre-Production/Set up	Pre-Production/Set up
10:00am-11:15am		<u>AEA Meeting</u> FULL COMPANY	
11:15am-12:00pm	<u>Meet and Greet</u> FULL COMPANY		
12:00pm-1:30pm	<u>REHEARSAL w/Grandage</u> FULL COMPANY		
1:30pm-2:30pm	LUNCH	<u>MUSIC w/Blodgette</u> R.Martin *(lunch 2-3pm)	LUNCH
2:30pm-4:30pm	<u>MUSIC w/</u> <u>Blodgete,Waldrop</u> *Requiem, Oh What A Circus* FULL ENSEMBLE		2:30-4:00pm <u>SCENE WORK w/Grandage</u> E.Roger, M.Cerveris, C.DeCicco
2:30pm-6:00pm	DANCE w/Ashford *Buenos Aires* C.DeCicco, M.von Essen & FULL ENSEMBLE *E.Roger joins at 5:00pm*		4:00-5:00pm <u>MUSIC w/</u> <u>Grandage, Blodgette</u> E.Roger
			5:00-6:00pm <u>MUSIC w/</u> <u>Grandage,Blodgette,</u> M.Martin, M.Cerveris
6:00pm	END OF DAY	END OF DAY	END OF DAY

<u>FITTINGS</u>
R.Eichenberger fitting 6:00-7:30pm at Studio, 555 8th ave,(bet 37th & 38th)

You can see there is a union meeting, a "meet and greet" and then rehearsal with the director in the morning. In the afternoon, everyone will learn some music and then choreography. It looks as though they will be doing one of the biggest dance numbers in the show. You will want to be prepared, physically and vocally, for these rehearsals.

If you take a look at the "Fittings" at the bottom, you see that Rebecca (R. Eichenberger) has a fitting at 6:00pm. She will likely have to leave 15-20 minutes early, so her swing should keep track of her in the dance to be able to step in when she leaves. Her swing may be learning new things in her place, or she may have to be in her place for the whole number if the choreographer decided to run the number at the end of the day. If you have to step in to learn new material for a performer, then just concentrate on learning that one person. Fill in the gaps, regarding the rest of your actors, during a break. You can ask the other swings or dance captain for help in looking at their notation afterward.

Every show does the first day of rehearsal differently. There will probably be a short "meet and greet" at the beginning of the day. This may consist of the director and designers talking through the show. You may meet the creative team and the producers. There will likely be a union meeting with a union representative who will give you particular union information and make sure you have signed and submitted your contract.

Sometimes, a show will do a "table read" on the first day. A table read is where the company sits around a table and reads (and perhaps sings) through the entire show. This gives everyone a chance to hear it before working on it. Sometimes, it is done later in the week instead, if the creative team wants to get some work done before doing the table read.

Here's another example of a **First Day Rehearsal Schedule:**

FIRST DAY Rehearsal SCHEDULE

	Studio A	Studio B	Studio C
10:00am-11:00am		AEA meeting FULL COMPANY	
11:00am-1:00pm	"Meet and Greet" FULL COMPANY		
1:00pm-2:00pm	Lunch	Lunch	Lunch
2:00pm-3:30pm		TABLE READ FULL COMPANY	
3:30-6:00pm	Start staging Act 1 FULL COMPANY		

In the above example, the full company will work in Studio A, staging the opening number in the afternoon. It is a musical, and there will probably be some movement or full dancing in the opening number. It's a good idea to wear dance clothes or clothes you can move in, as well as a pair of shoes you can dance in. You may want to come a bit early to warm up your body and muscles in preparation for the afternoon rehearsal.

You Teach People How to Treat You

Where you physically place yourself in the room, to write down information, will set a precedent for where the company can expect you to be for the rest of your rehearsal process. If you confidently go to the front of the room, then people will expect you there in the future and you won't be "in the way". If you start the process by trying to slink around "invisibly" and be out of everyone's way, then that is where you will be expected to be. Always be mindful of letting the choreographer and director do their job, but be confident that you have a job to do and it's in everyone's best interest for you to be in the best possible position to do your job. You are starting the process of teaching people how to treat you.

Some stage managers will automatically place a "swing table" at the front of the room so the swings have some place to work while getting all the information they need.

If there is no swing table, you can ask stage management for one. If there is not enough room, you can grab a chair and a music stand and make your own place to work. You may even want to label the chair and music stand so no one sits in it and are guaranteed to have your special spot whenever you need it.

Sleep is your Friend

You will never be more tired than when you are learning a show. You are using all of your muscles, memory included, to "the max". You must treat your body well. It will help your ability to learn and perform your job the best. Just remember that this part of the process is temporary.

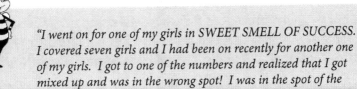

"*I went on for one of my girls in SWEET SMELL OF SUCCESS. I covered seven girls and I had been on recently for another one of my girls. I got to one of the numbers and realized that I got mixed up and was in the wrong spot! I was in the spot of the other girl, who was onstage with me and not the spot I was covering that show. Luckily, she had been a swing before and saw what was going on. She just moved over to fill in the spot where I should have been. It's nice when actors can just adjust and not make a scene versus panic and make you feel badly for being in their spot.*" - Lisa Gajda

"*I understand that swinging isn't always for everyone. I actually really enjoy it. I love the variety. I love getting to go on for parts/features I wouldn't normally be cast in. I love saving the day. One aspect of swinging that I don't enjoy quite so much are the props. Props stress me out. One number that comes to mind is 'Company Way' from HOW TO SUCCEED IN BUSINESS WITHOUT REALLY TRYING. Set in a mailroom, four of my first covers were dancing mail room workers. The number looked amazing. There were flying packages going everywhere. Hampers spinning, with people standing and jumping on them. Intricate envelope choreography with partners. Super athletic. It was awesome. It was also my biggest nightmare. It required my thinking cap, especially stepping into a track for the first time in a while. The four gents had similar responsibilities, but each were different enough that going on autopilot could never be an option or it would all end in tears. I think the other boys found it entertaining when I was on because they knew how I felt about this number. A topic of conversation in the wings right before we entered would often be if "MJ is going to catch the package today." Basically, two of the boys would slide under the counter to grab a package with their feet, pull themselves up onto the counter and toss their legs like a scorpion with the box in their feet to toss it forward towards the audience, and the other two boys would jump up and catch it. It's live theatre. It's a hard thing to do. The box wouldn't always go straight. You have to adapt. No matter how hard I tried, more often than not, the package would end up anywhere but in my hands. Often our conductor would be conducting, see it headed in his direction and either catch it and toss it back to me or give it a sensible volleyball hit my way. It's those moments as a swing that you just have to laugh off and not let it ruin your show. Embrace it, and move on.*" - Michaeljon Slinger

CHAPTER 10

Rehearsals

Rehearsals for a New Show

You will continue to learn new vocal parts, lyrics, choreography, lines and staging daily. You want to keep on top of any script changes. It helps to come in a few minutes early to check your mailbox to see what changes have been made from the day before. It's essential to take a moment at the beginning of the day and put those changes into your current score/script. The creative team and writers work very hard making improvements every night after the cast goes home. Someone has to print and distribute all the new information. It makes the creative team upset when you don't keep up to date on new material. It doesn't look good when you say an old script line when they have taken the time to re-write it.

You will have written important information in your script and score. Instead of throwing away the old one with this information on it, just fold the old page in half, length wise, and put the new page behind it. When you have time, go back and transfer your notes to the new page. You may want to delay this process because it's not uncommon for there to be many revisions to the same page before it's finalized. There have been times when the writers decide to try something and then go back to the old way. If you don't have notes written on the old page, you can recycle the old page and get it out of your binder.

Here's an example of what to do when you get new pages:

Strike a line through the old page. Fold and keep it on top of the new page.

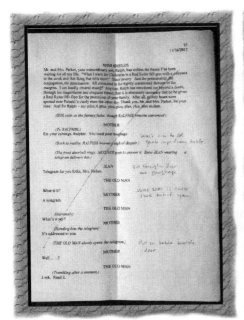 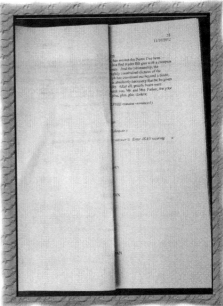

Rehearsal Run-Throughs

Once the show has been roughly staged and choreographed, you will be asked to do run-throughs. There may be a time during a run-through when they send someone for a wardrobe, shoe, or wig fitting. It's a good idea to look on the callboard or ask the stage manager the day before a run-through so you can be prepared. If you are told that someone will be out, then look through your notes and make a cheat sheet. Include the name of the scene, entrances, exits, who you partner with and what props you use. It's helpful to write down what scenes are in-between so you know how long you have until the next time you appear. There may be holes in your information. Make a list of questions to ask the person you are covering before they are pulled away.

There may be more than one person gone in one day. Write a cheat sheet for anybody who will be out. Even though you think someone will only be out for one number, write down more than that because you never know when he or she will be back.

Here's an example of a "cheat sheet" during rehearsals.

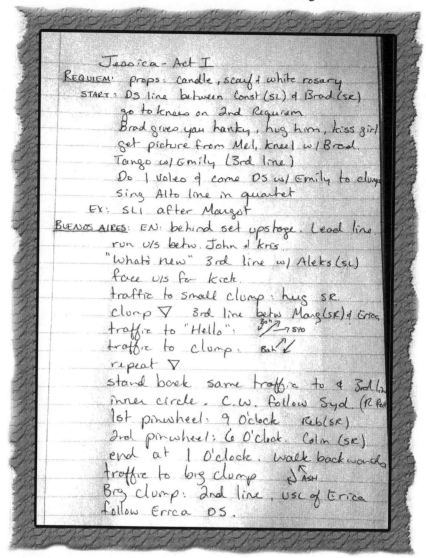

Just breathe!

This is one of the hardest times in the process because everything is so new to everyone. Just do your best, and that will be good enough. Even though it's nerve-racking and you feel very vulnerable because you want to do a good job, it's a good thing to get experience with the cast. It's how you learn. So, embrace those difficult moments; keep a smile on your face and a good attitude. Tomorrow is another day.

Rehearsals for an Existing Show

Rehearsing for an existing show is a much easier process than rehearsing for a new show. If a show is already running, then everything is "set" or "frozen". They know exactly what you should be doing at all times. You will go into a studio with the dance captain and/or the stage manager and be taught the entire show.

The more difficult part regarding this process is you don't have the luxury of having many other people to interact with in your rehearsal process. You may feel more vulnerable because you might be the only person singing or dancing at any given time. You have to go over your vocal harmonies and lyrics so you can focus on learning the choreography quickly in the studio.

Tech Rehearsals for a New Show

If you are rehearsing a new show, you will go into the theatre to "tech" the show before it opens to the public. Before going into the theater, ask the stage manager if you and the other swings can get a "swing table". There will be a lot going on in all departments, and everyone will be pushed to their limits. You can give yourself an advantage by speaking with the stage managers before you leave the studio, so they can have time to arrange it. If you wait until you are in the theatre, it may be too hectic for the stage manager to deal with it in a timely fashion.

Each department has a portable table in the "house" during tech rehearsals. You will have a lot of work to do, and you should have the same benefit. The table needs lights and a power source for your computers. The table sits above a row of theatre seats and a long bench is place over another row of seats to allow you to sit at the table. Just like theatre seating, you will only be able to access the table from either side of the row of seats. You will need to get up from the table a lot, so make sure there aren't too many people placed at your table. The stage manager may put dance captains and understudies at the table with you. Keep in communication with the stage manager about whether there is enough room for you to get your job done.

First Day of Tech at the Theatre

When you arrive, look for the callboard and sign-in. There will probably be a lot of valuable information on the board for you to read. This information will include dressing room assignments, a schedule for the day, and where and when the full cast meets. Give yourself a few extra minutes on the first day to find your dressing room and get settled in.

Stay off the stage until the stage manager calls you to the stage. The crew is probably working hard in order to get everything done before the cast steps onstage. They need time and space to do so. They also want to make sure the area is safe before you step onto the stage. You can wait in your dressing room, backstage or in the house until you are called over the PA system by your stage manager.

The stage manager will ask the cast to gather on stage or in the house. They will probably take you on a mini tour of the theatre to get you acquainted with it. The stage manager may ask you to "mic up" and will tell you where you should do so.

Getting "Mic'd up"

Every show handles microphones for swings differently. Once the onstage cast has "mic'd up", you can ask the sound person at the table what they want to do with swings. It's good to be prepared for occasions when you get asked to go on in a moment's notice. It takes a little bit of time to fit the elastic, find an extra mic chord that matches your hair or wig, and to find a mic belt that fits you. You want to discuss all of this before you actually need it.

You probably will not put a mic on during tech rehearsals unless you have your own or unless you have to go on for someone. Again, you can just ask the sound person how they want to work with swings.

What to Wear to Tech Rehearsals

All actors have learned over the years not to wear white or bright colors to tech. It's important to wear black or dark colors because the lighting department is creating the lighting effects. White and light colors bounce the light and make it difficult for them to do their job. If you do wear light clothing, you will probably be asked to change into something dark. Some shows now are asking you to wear costumes for tech. Light and white *costumes* are fine, as the lighting department will get a chance to see what the actual show will look like in the lighting they create.

Making the Most of your Tech Time

The stage manager will probably start "teching" at the top of the show the first day in the theatre. It's probably best not to go on the stage while they are positioning the actors unless you are having difficulty seeing the numbers where people are placed. Usually, they will have large temporary numbers across the front of the stage so you can see it while sitting in the house. Find a place where you can see and hear what is being said to the cast, and write down all the changes.

You can start by sitting in the house to get all the information you need. If not, you will have to find another way to get it done. After all, you need to be able to do your job well, and the whole company benefits. One option is to go to the wings and try to get information that way. The crew will also be in the wings trying to learn their show, so be mindful of allowing them to do their job. You can also stand onstage briefly in the back or front just to get spacing, but be aware that the choreographer or director may want to move quickly, and they may want to see the full picture with just the onstage cast. Take the "temperature" of the room as to when you should be on the stage or in the wings.

If you are not getting the information you need and feel uncomfortable with how to go about it, just have a conversation with the stage manager or the dance captain on the break. They are your allies and understand how important it is for you to get all the information you need. They can always have conversations with the choreographer or director in order to come up with a system where everyone is happy. Sometimes, the dance captain has more leeway to get up on the stage and can perhaps help give you more specific information once he/she gets it all down. Often, the choreographer or director will stage a picture, and then there will be some time after where everyone stands still while the lighting department programs their cues. This may be a great time to get up on the stage and notate what you need.

Grab your clipboard, a pencil/eraser, the charts you made in the rehearsal studio and some new, blank charts. The best way to mark actors' new positions is to cross out the old notation (rather than erase it) and write in a new one beside it. This is helpful when the choreographer says "Why isn't this picture working? What number were you in the studio?" The actor may have been moved from SL5 to SL8 when they were placed on stage. Sometimes the choreographer will play with a picture and then go back to what it was before.

Find out what the stage manager, creative team and dance captain are calling each exit so all of you are using the same terms. This will make notation easier in the long run. For example, if they call the exits A,B,C and D, it will make it more difficult if you call them 1,2,3, and 4. It may work for your system but will pose more complications when communicating with other cast members and the creative team.

The breaks may be your best (and only) chance to get on the stage and try things. That could mean practicing choreography or just orienting yourself on the stage. Always ask the stage manger first if it is okay for you to go on the stage to try something. You will not be able to touch the sets or props because the union crews are also on break. If you need to touch a set piece or prop, tell the stage manager, and they will find the appropriate time for you to do so.

These are the days that there will be "down time" between numbers and you will have a chance to catch up on things. Once a number has been lit and staged, the creative team will move to the next number. If you are not involved in the current number they are teching, use that time to clean up your notes. It's a good time to make a new set of charts that are clean and easy to read with the new information on them. Keep the old ones and just staple them together. Put a pencil slash across it or write "draft" so you know it is not the most current information. You can label it "studio" or write the date so you can remind yourself what those charts were for. You probably have some important notes on those original charts so you keep them. You may not want to transfer all those notes to the new charts quite yet as there may still be changes. As you continue with the process of tech and previews, you may have to write a whole new set of charts if the creative team wants to change things. They will continue to change and tweak things until opening night.   Once they are done "teching" one number, put your charts in your binder and get ready for the next number.

The biggest change from the studio rehearsals to the stage is the backstage and wing area. As the show is being "teched", there is a lot of "offstage choreography" that gets figured out at the same time. It's important to be present or nearby when these things are figured out so you know what to do when you go on. Write down the wings everyone enters and exits from and in what order.   Write down what props will be used and where the actors get them and return them to.

If it is too crowded backstage during tech, then forgo all the prop and backstage details until they are ironed out. You can always ask someone later. There is usually a stage manager assigned to each side of the stage in charge of everything on that side. They will have a good idea how crowded it is. Always check with them first to let them know you are there, or ask them if it is okay for you to be there. They know what set pieces and props need to move and will always look out for your safety and tell you where the best place is to stand.

The tech process is a lot slower than the rehearsal process. You want to get as much information down as you can because it may be a while before you "revisit" it.   You are still responsible for knowing it.

Sometimes, if there is going to be a lot of time between certain numbers, the choreographer may ask for the company to go to a studio or location to review or learn choreography. Always go with the chorus when called, and leave the chart clean up for a "free moment".

There will probably not be many of those "free moments" for the swings. There is much to keep on top of that you should always make use of your time during tech rehearsal to learn all of your tracks (cleaning charts, going over choreography, writing it down, refreshing vocals, words and harmonies, and grabbing partners to work with). Do the most work you can during the day, so you can go home and relax. The downtime at home is precious and will help make you a more effective swing.

During tech rehearsals, keep an eye on the wardrobe, shoe and wig calls to make sure you are prepared to go on for that person. Now that the cast is in the building, these departments may try to pull people away briefly without a schedule.

Here is a recap of what to do during tech rehearsals:

- *Ask stage management for a swing table in the house.*
- *Stay off the stage until called by stage management.*
- *Wait until the cast "mic'd up", then ask the sound department about swings.*
- *Wear dark colors for the lighting department.*
- *Make sure you are using the same lingo and terms as everyone else.*
- *Ask stage management anytime you want to be in the wings while they are working.*
- *Use the breaks to your advantage and orient yourself to the stage and backstage.*
- *Keep a list of things you need to do or touch before going on for someone.*
- *Use the "down time" to catch up and get prepared for the next scene.*
- *Watch for fittings on the schedule so you are prepared to go on.*
- *Getting all the new information is imperative to doing a great job.*

Here is a recap of how to get all the information you need:

- *Start by sitting in the House.*
- *Take the "temperature" of the room, and get on the stage when you can.*
- *Get in the wings and notate the "offstage choreography".*
- *Write everything down (make sure you have a lot of paper/charts on hand).*
- *Keep your old charts and create new ones as you go along.*
- *Have a discussion with the stage manager or dance captain if you aren't feeling like you are getting everything down you need to do your job well.*

Tech Rehearsals for an Existing Show

Technical rehearsals for an existing show are much different. The show has already been "teched", and you are the only one that needs to be put into the show. During your rehearsal process (usually 2 weeks), you will get onstage and be able to use the props, see the scenery and perhaps see how it moves. You will likely have a put-in with most of the company. The level of technical aspects that will be used differs from show to show. You may or may not have your mic, costumes, wigs, or have lights and moving scenery. It is costly to recreate what happens during a show, so the stage manager, along with the general manager, will decide what aspects are needed for you. It will depend on safety issues and cost.

The Sitzprobe

This is when the cast gets the chance to sit with the orchestra and sing. It is a German opera term that literally means "seated rehearsal". This usually involves sitting in the lobby, onstage or in a studio. The cast will be in folding chairs with a number of microphones lined up in front of the chairs. The musicians will be seated and ready to play. It's the first chance the cast hears what the orchestra will sound like, and it's the first time the orchestra hears the cast. No costumes are worn. No staging or dancing is done. This is the musical director's time, and he/she will be in charge. You can wear comfortable clothes. You are welcome to bring your score/script with you to follow along. You will not go through the entire show, just the numbers where the orchestra and vocals work together. This may be the only time you get to see the musicians as they play. It is a very exciting part of the rehearsal process. Bring your cameras and recording devices, if you are permitted. Everyone will be asked to sing full out. If there are soloists, they will be told to come to a microphone to sing. When the chorus sings, you may be asked to group around the microphones, or you may be asked to sing from where you are seated and allow the soloists to come to the mics.

Dress Rehearsal

This can be a stressful time if costumes have not been used during any part of the rehearsal or tech process. Costumes can change the timing of transitions, the sound, and the partnering. It's a great time to stay out of the way and let everyone work out the kinks. You can always shadow backstage at another time to see how things are done.

If it's a REALLY important change that you are worried about or know you will have to go on for soon, then ask a stage manager if you can watch what is going on and tell him/her what your concerns are. He/she will figure out if it is a good time or he/she will schedule a time for you to learn the specifics.

This may be a good time to watch the run-through from a different area of the house. It's good to sit in the mezzanine or balcony to get a bird's-eye-view of patterns and such.

Video taping is not officially allowed without proper permission and notice. This is to protect union workers: actors, designers, and creatives. Limited taping can be done to help you do your job, but it will not be allowed when the show has an audience. Use the time in rehearsals wisely, and obtain any important information you need, such as entrances, exits, traffic patterns, timing, partnering lifts and poses. You can use a flip, PDA (personal digital assistant) or hand-held device. It's good to tape the front of your device if it has a red recording light so it's not distracting to the cast members. Try and be inconspicuous because it's not widely appreciated. Although it does help you tremendously with your job as a swing, be respectful of the footage and don't use it for purposes other than your job. It's not meant for the web or other public avenues. Remember, early press can kill a show, and that includes your job too. It is frowned upon from unions in order to protect the actor's, director's, choreographer's and designer's work.

"PIRATE QUEEN - Wednesday matinee and one of the actors had jury duty. They thought he would make it in time for the show, but luckily I asked if I could step in for him at fight call as I had never been on for this track. Half hour call came and went; finally, at 15 they decided to put me on. This track was not particularly difficult, but did involve non-stop costume changes in the second act - none of which we had time to go over because they weren't even sure what I would be wearing. I went into every change not knowing if the next costume would even fit. My dresser was a nervous wreck, and I had to stay calm for both of us. As a swing, it is so important to stay focused, even when everyone around you is flipping out." - Jeff Williams

"I was a swing for HOW TO SUCCEED IN BUSINESS WITHOUT REALLY TRYING, and I was scheduled to go on for a track I had never done before. The number 'Stop that man' started with all the men spaced on a 3 story scaffolding, and they made their way to different quadrants of the scaffolding, throughout the number. This actor started 3 stories high and made his way down to the bottom during the number. I had a rehearsal scheduled the morning I was going on, to try my choreography on the set. The night before, there was a huge snowstorm, and the theatre's skylight shattered. There was snow and glass all over the set, so they had to cancel our rehearsal to clean it up before the show. It was a good thing that I was not afraid of heights, because the first time I went on for this track was in front of a sold out audience, with no rehearsal on the set." - Karl Warden

"One night at EVITA, about 5 minutes before the show was to start, my friend threw up in the bathroom. She got a very sudden stomach virus. She had also previously been a swing, so she came running out of the bathroom crying as she said to me, 'I'm sorry, I have to call out'. My first thought was 'Of course, I hope you get better soon'. My second thought was 'Holy crap! I have to run and get ready! This is the first time I have done her track! I won't have time to practise my dance lifts with my partners! I have a dance feature with Ricky Martin in the second act! The director is in the audience tonight! Tonight of all nights!'" I ran to my dressing room. I reviewed my notes as I shoved my hair into my prep. Everyone wanted to talk to me to see how I was feeling and all I wanted to do was cry and stop the clock. I just wanted more time to prepare. The show started at a funeral, where we could cry ...and boy, did I! I got it all out in that number, and then I told myself to just be present and enjoy the moment. The partnering with Ricky was a blast! I got an email from the director afterwards saying he admired what I did that night. It was 'focused, characterful, and committed'." - Jennie Ford

"I recall my first Broadway show where one of the swings came to 'places' and told everyone to 'shove with love'. I felt that it was such an awesome way to tell everyone to push him gently into place if he seemed in the way, but to be mindful of doing it with kindness." - Anonymous

"I remember my first time on in THE MUSIC MAN. The entire cast had to learn how to play trombones for the 'Finale Ultimo'. It began with a 30 second **full** costume change. Then everyone grabbed a trombone and marched onstage to do the choreography. **Everything** was choreographed, including trombone slide positions, and knowing when to put your thumb on the mouthpiece to avoid it falling out or locking your slide. I went on for the first time and my whole family was in the audience for the occasion. The show went well for me until the last number when I had to swing my trombone up to make part of a tunnel for the lead, Harold Hill, to walk through for his bow. I forgot to lock my slide! As I swung my trombone around and up, my slide went flying up in the air and into the wings! Then after Harold bows, we pay a jazzy version of '76 trombones'. I had to pretend I was playing and I felt like an idiot because I was missing my whole trombone slide while playing." - Cynthia Leigh Heim

CHAPTER 11

It's Showtime!

Previews

Previews are shows for the public before the official opening. The purpose of previews is to allow the creative team to identify problems and opportunities for improvement that weren't evident during rehearsals. Adjustments are made before critics are invited to attend. This is a very busy time for everyone. Even though you have a show every night, rehearsals are happening each day, with many changes. You have to be on top of those changes and be ready to go on for any of the performers you cover. Everyone is exhausted and more prone to injuries and illness.

You need to make sure you get a look at what is going on backstage during a show. You will need to know everything, such as: quick-changes, where they get props and where they return them, where they crossover, and how to maneuver around backstage scenery that is constantly moving during the show. Talk to your stage manager to schedule when you can do that. It may be best to schedule an overall viewing of backstage during the show so you can observe what a number of your tracks do. You can also choose to trail one person. You will be solid on that one person, but not comfortable if someone else goes out. It may be best to get an overall view before you track individually. You can ask individuals in the dressing room for specific helpful hints such as "Where do you grab your hanky? Who do you follow when you enter? How do you avoid the oncoming scenery for that number?"

This is a good time to start making individual track sheets or books if you haven't already. (See Chapter 13 on creating your swing books) Keep everything in pencil and remain flexible, knowing that nothing is frozen until opening night and will likely change. You have to have something to refer to when you go on for someone during previews.

Be Prepared To Go On Anytime

Now that the show is open to the public, you have to be ready to go on for any of the people you cover. You have to be "show ready", and there are many things you can do to help yourself be prepared.

> *TIP:*
> *Now is the time to make sure the stage managers' numbers are programmed into your cell phone. They will likely try to text you if something was to happen during a show, and they need you to come backstage and get ready to go on. You don't want to miss any call or text from a stage manager!*

Keep a list of things you would need to try if you were to go on for each of the tracks you cover. Talk with your stage manager, and see if there is anything you could do ahead of time. This will prevent you from cramming everything in before you go on. In some cases, you could be thrown on during a show without having the chance to rehearse. It's better to get as much done beforehand so you feel comfortable. Such things could include partnering, cartwheels off tables, walking on a treadmill or turntable, walking high on scaffolding, sliding down a fireman's pole, touching props that are time-specific in the show, moving scenery or props, trying your show shoes on the deck surface, using costume pieces and show shoes while partnering or working with set pieces or props.

During the preview shows, you will have the opportunity to watch the shows or be backstage. Do whatever helps you get prepared to go on. Both watching and observing backstage are extremely helpful, and a combination of both is the best. If you are watching a show, let a stage manager know where you will be and how they can contact you if someone goes out. It happens!

When the cast is rehearsing costume, you will most likely not be in costume. The cast and dressers need that time to work things out on their own without adding more bodies. This makes it difficult for you to have the proper time to work in the costumes, shoes and wigs you will be performing in. If you are really concerned about something, write it down and bring it up with the stage manager. They may schedule some time for you to be in costume and shoes to try things ahead of time. If not, then just keep a list for when you have to go on for someone, and they will make time for you before the show. These are "best efforts" though. There may be the odd time where someone gets hurt or sick during a show and you have to go on. You will not have time to rehearse these things, so it's always good to get as much done as possible prior.

You must start to create a system to help prepare you for when you go on for each track. Your system is unique to you, and so is the method you learn and retain things. There are ways to do it, such as making individual track sheets or individual books. Refer to Chapter 13 on how to make your swing books, to determine what system suits you. Keep in mind things will be changing, so it's too soon for a *permanent* system.

Anticipate

After the show opens to the public, you want to make sure you are prepared to go on. This includes helping *other* departments get prepared for when you go on. You don't want to be thrown on and have all the departments vying for your time while you should be looking over your notes. It's very stressful if everything is left until last minute!

WARDROBE: Make sure you know what you will be wearing for each person you cover and every number they are in. Will you wear your own costume or something you share with someone that needs to be fitted for you? Wardrobe may find they need to make something or possibly buy or pull something from stock. Talk through any costume quick changes you are worried about. Is it different from what the dressers are used to? Do your shoes need dance rubber on the bottom of them? Do your shoes need to be rigged with quick-change buckles on them?

HAIR: Have you tried on all your wigs yet? This is a great time to talk to the hair supervisor to schedule a wig fitting. You will put your hair into a wig prep and then try on your wigs. Not all of them will be perfect when they are put on your head. Some will need to be loosened, tightened or restyled to suit your face. This takes time, and it's good to give the hair department ample time to take care of these things. It's also important to fit your wig with a mic pack or something to take the place of it if you wear your microphone in your wig. It may seem like a small detail, but it makes a difference if the wig is tight and the lace is pulling. For the men, facial hair should be tried on, too.

SETS: Are there some set pieces you still need to see or get on in order to properly cover someone's track? (Sliding down a pole, cartwheel off a table, walking on a treadmill, jumping off a step, getting inside a set piece for staging) All this should be done ahead of time. It may also involve paying crew members. The stage manager may want to do this during a rehearsal when the crew is already called.

PROPS: Are there props you need to touch and get used to? You won't be able to just pick them up and try them any time you want. Make a list, and talk with stage management about the best time to try them.

SOUND: You should figure out where you would like to wear your microphone during the show. There are many factors that go into deciding this: partnering, tight costumes and comfort. Once you decide where you want to wear it, make sure your undergarments or costumes are ready for your microphone during a performance. For example, you may need a mic belt or a holder sewn into your costume or undergarments.

PARTNERING: Have you had the chance to partner with the actors you will be partnering during the show? If there are things you are nervous about or need practice, just ask the dance captain or the actor if you can partner with them. Some actors are fine if you approach them directly, and some are not. No matter what, for safety reasons, a dance captain should be present when you rehearse partnering and lifts.

INDIVIDUAL BOOKS: It is helpful to make individual books or track sheets for each person so everything is easy to read and carry with you backstage when you need it. You can go to the drugstore or an office supply store and purchase coiled index cards. Create a book for each person, including charts, choreography, props, costumes, changes, vocal harmonies and anything else you will need. (see Chapter 14 on creating swing books)

TIP:
Writing down things to remember can be a bigger deal than you think!

One swing went onstage and forgot to move his mic pack from his back to his hip. He did a forward roll in one of the numbers and damaged one of his vertebrae.

During a Show

When you are on for someone, they likely have a specific place to change into costume with a specific dresser. They may have a specific quick-change area, a specific place to get their mic and a specific time for wig changes. Generally, you would do whatever they do, because the crew that assists them has other duties that are choreographed as well. Sometimes you are able to stay in your own dressing room and everyone adjusts to you. Ask your stage manager about this in advance.

Questions to ask: Will I stay at my dressing spot or move to the other actor's spot? Do I have different costumes than the actor I am replacing, and do I need to address it with his/her dresser? Where will the sound department put my mic when I go on for another actor?

You get "The Call"

The phone rings.
You see it's stage management.
Your heart races.
You answer.
You are told you are on for "........."
Tell the stage manager if there is anything you will need before going on.
You prepare all the way until showtime.
The curtain goes up.
You think of nothing else in your life but that moment in this show.
The curtain comes down.
Everybody cheers and congratulates you.

Opening Night

Opening night is an exciting time for everyone. More than likely, you will not be on this night. Some swings are okay with this, and some have a harder time. Just remember, you will be able to get ready for the party and not worry about show hair and make up! It's a time to look at the positive...you will look like a million bucks!

Every cast member is allowed a certain number of tickets...usually two. You will want to decide what you will be doing that night. The choices are either sitting in the theatre to watch or staying backstage. If you want to sit, then talk to your company manager way ahead of time to let them know your wishes. Make sure they have a seat for you as well as your two guests, like the rest of the cast. If you don't, they will give that seat away and there will be nowhere for you to sit on opening night. If you get a seat for yourself, you are not guaranteed to sit with your guests.

Shows After Opening Night

Here it is! The moment you have been waiting for. The show is frozen, the director and choreographer have left, and now you are the one to save the show when someone calls out. It's time to be prepared for anything!

Your "Put-In"

If you have a scheduled performance when you know you are going on, you will likely get a "put-in". This will give you the opportunity to experience what performing the show feels like before you do it in front of an audience. You will likely have a put-in with most of the company. The level of technical aspects that will be used differs from show to show. You may or may not be wearing a microphone, your costumes or wigs, or have lights or moving scenery. It is costly to recreate what happens during a show, so the stage manager, along with the general manager, will decide what aspects are needed for you. It will depend on safety issues and cost. Any rehearsal onstage with technical elements is beneficial. Just appreciate what you are given, and know there will always be aspects you will experience for the first time when you perform live in front of an audience.

Split Tracks

There may be a show where more than one person you cover is absent. You may be asked to cover two or more people during one show. This is called a "split track". The dance captain, with the help of the stage manager, will decide what are the most important or necessary elements of each track and combine the tracks to come up with what you should do for that show. This is not something that happens all the time and no two combinations are ever the same, so it's important to review this "split track" and make sure it works. You can help the dance captain and stage manager by coming up with what you think works best for you or reviewing what they have come up with to make sure they haven't missed anything. Not only do you have to consider onstage choreography, but you have to consider entrances and exits, costume changes, the time needed to go from one place to another. They may need you to be one person in the first scene and another in the second scene, but the two actors may exit and enter on opposite sides. If there is no time to cross over, you will have to alter your entrances and exits to make it work. All of this needs to be communicated to the cast and crew departments so everyone knows what to expect.

"There was one show where the stomach flu ran through the company. It seemed like everyone was calling out. The stage manager phoned to tell me I would be on for one of my tracks that night. He also said that one girl called to say she was sick but would see how she was feeling later that day. The other female swing was already scheduled to be on for one of her tracks. Then he called and said I would be doing a split track between two girls. Then he called back to say that yet another girl called out of the show. I had no idea how we were going to do the show with so many people out. The stage manager then called back to say that one of the girls didn't seem as sick as the others, so she would try to come in and do the show. We did the best we could to cover everything, and 'the show went on' that night." - Jennie Ford

It's a good idea to have the particular "split-track" written out so you can quickly see what to expect next. You don't want to wait for the middle of the show to realize you should have asked a question or realize that something does not work.

Keep a record of the split tracks you do. It may come in handy if you ever have to do it again. It's not something you will do regularly. It's easy to forget what you did last time, particularly if it was 6 months ago.

Attitude and Energy

One of the most important characteristics of a good swing is a good temperament. You can be the most talented person on the planet, but you need the right personality to be a swing. The best thing you can do for yourself and the company is remain calm and keep a sense of humor. There is no constructive use for displaying stress or whining. Yes, your job is hard! Yes, everyone does appreciate your job! Yes, it may "suck to be you" right now, but think of it as an opportunity to affect people in a positive way. Your cast mates are your cheerleaders. They want you to succeed and they are thrilled there is a new person on stage to "play" with.

You will make mistakes. You can't judge yourself more harshly than you would any friend going through what you are going through right now. Be a friend to yourself. Laugh, and learn from your mistakes. Smile through your stress, and you will see the whole theatre relieved to have you save the day. Doing your best is all that you can ask of yourself.

Enjoy this ride and journey of self-discovery. Push yourself to the limit, and see what that feels like. Test your memory, knowing that it's healthy for your mind. Test your physical body, and attack stress head-on with open arms. You will never replace that amazing feeling, when the curtain goes down and the cast cheers. It is for you, your talent, your efforts and your bravery that they cheer! Revel in it. Congratulate yourself. Learn from your mistakes, knowing that the next time will be even better. Appreciate what many people "would kill" to experience!

"I was swinging CATS and 'Tumblebrutus' cut his finger on a set piece during one number. He was supposed to do the 'Victoria lift', but she was wearing a white unitard, and he was bleeding. He didn't want to get blood all over it. I was already onstage for one of my other tracks, so he made his way over to me during the number and told me to fill in for his lift. I left my partner to improv by herself in the dark, and I made my way over for the lift. I was two feet taller than the Tumblebrutus so when Victoria turned around, she saw my chest and her face panned up to my face with slight surprise. I lifted her so high in the air for the overhead split lift that she said, 'Weeeeee'. Tumblebrutus went offstage to get a bandage during the number. He returned, and I returned to my partner."
- Karl Warden

CHAPTER 12

The "Perks" of a Broadway Show

The TONY Awards

This is the highest honor in live theatre in the United States. Some shows are asked to perform during the live telecast event. It will mostly be comprised of shows that have been nominated in categories such as Best Musical or Choreography. Depending on what number is picked, you may or may not be asked to perform. It comes down to advertising and the cost of doing business.

Everyone gets paid on a SAG-AFTRA contract because it's television. It costs the producers money to have the cast perform a number from the show. They are hoping that the viewers will like what they see and buy tickets. Some creative teams and producers feel that the swings add more bodies onstage and make the production number look great!

Once a show gets asked to perform on the TONYS, the creative team will figure out the best number and if the swings will be included. Your family and friends back home can tune in to watch you on television. You will receive a separate check for your rehearsals and your performance on the TONYS. There will be a rehearsal at the theatre for the specific TONY performance. You will go to a studio and record the vocals separately. There will be a rehearsal on the TONY stage during the days leading up to the TONYS.

On the day of the show, you will have a dress rehearsal during the day. You will get ready at the theatre, get on a bus, drive to the TONY theatre, wait to be called off the bus, wait in a holding tent, make your way to the stage to rehearse, exit immediately to the bus and drive back to the theatre. That night, during the show, you will do the same thing again. You won't be able to see the show while it is running. Often, someone at the theatre will tune a TV into the TONYS while you get ready for your own performance. When you wait in the holding tent, you can see on the big screens what is going on in the theatre. You will usually see the number before you as well as some presenters' speeches. You may not even hear the winner of your category announced because you are on a bus or back at your show's theatre.

Some producers host a TONY viewing party during/after the show so the cast has somewhere to be together to watch. After your performance, you change back into regular clothes at the theatre and head to the party. They will likely show your performance at that venue if they have the capability.

TV Shows

The producers will hire a theatrical press agency to help them promote and advertise the show. They may reach out to television programming or TV shows (Good Morning America, Rosie O'Donell, The Today Show, David Letterman, Dancing with the Stars, and The View to name a few, past and present). The TV show may request something or the producers will suggest what they want. They will decide who they will use from the company. It could be it's just a few principals; sometimes it is some of the chorus; and sometimes it's everyone, including the swings. It costs the producers money, so they have to determine how many people watch that show, what time it will be on, and how it will help ticket sales.

These shows will be on a SAG-AFTRA contract as well with the applicable rates. The contract will depend on how long the show is that you are performing on, how many people will be performing and what role you play in the number. You will have separate rehearsals at your theatre and on the show's stage. You will likely do a blocking rehearsal for the cameras on the day before or the day of the show. You may or may not do a dress rehearsal. Sometimes you will change at the theatre and sometimes you will change at the venue.

Commercials

Some producers do a commercial that is specific for their show. It could be something the producers create out of the captured B-roll. They could also choose to shoot something new and bring in special lights and cameras. You may be asked to go to a studio to record the vocals separately. This is done on a SAG-AFTRA contract if it is a commercial for radio and/or television.

The Cast Album

Not all shows do cast album recordings. Those that do, find a recording studio where the company goes over the course of one or two days. This will also be done on a SAG-AFTRA contract, but at a rate negotiated by AEA. The producers have to pay for the musicians, singers, engineers, and everyone else involved. They will decide if the swings will be used on the recording. It is a nice gesture because you wouldn't normally hear the swings' voices in addition to the onstage cast every night. It also costs more money. If you are included, thank those involved in the decision to have you on the album.

"The cast was so excited when we were told that we were going to record the album of our new Broadway show. It would take place on the day off. I asked our company manager if the swings would be involved, and he said he didn't know yet. Another month went by, and I asked again; still no answer. I turned down a reading on that day off, in the hopes that the swings would be included. About 6 days before the recording date, the company manager told us that we would not be included on the recording. It was so disappointing! I understood that including the swings wasn't expected, but I wish they had made the decision sooner, so I knew what to expect. Ultimately, it's the decision of the producers and general management, if they want to spend the money to include the swings, or not. It's important to have allies on the creative team or in stage management that can push for swings to be included. It's hard on the moral of the swings! You work so hard to save the show when you are needed, and some decisions don't come across as very appreciative or respectful of the swings' efforts!" - Anonymous

You will be given a list of what order the songs are to be recorded. You will be told to stand around a microphone and will be handed a headset. This headset is to hear the band (possibly in the other room) and what is being said from the booth. The purpose of the headphones is so you can hear the track you are singing to, but to avoid having the microphone pick up the background track. You can wear both sides of the headphones on your ears to get a clean track and avoid "bleed". The headphones allow the engineer to give you more background track or vocals while still getting a clean vocal track. Some singers like to keep a headphone on one ear and slide the other off the other ear so they can still hear themselves and the rest of the people in the room. It is important to make sure the other headphone is pressed against your cheek or head so the background track in the headphones cannot be heard by the microphone.

You also want to be quiet a few moments before and after each take so that you don't "chime in" and ruin a recorded take. If you have music, you want to put it on a stand and not shuffle the papers while the recording is happening in case the microphone picks it up. You can tell the engineer if your headphones aren't working properly, if you need more band, more click-track or if you need more of your own voice in your headphones. If you get a break while other cast members are still recording, take your headphones off and unplug them from the mixer box so no sound bleeds from them. Then plug them back in when you need it again.

Thanksgiving Day Parade

This is another special day of tradition and national pride in the United States. The Macy's parade is full of marching bands, balloons and handlers, floats with singers, variety acts and of course, Broadway show performances. The hour before the parade officially arrives at Macy's is when most of the Broadway show performances are aired (usually 9:00am-10:00am EST).

"I remember doing the Thanksgiving Day Parade during THE MUSIC MAN. A car came to pick me up at 4:00am, and it was still dark out. We got to the street in front of Macy's and each Broadway show took turns rehearsing outside in "just below freezing" temperatures. We were allowed to keep our coat, hats and gloves on for the first rehearsal. When it came time for camera rehearsal and the actual live portion, we had to take off our outer wear and dance in costume. We saw the 'Good Vibrations' cast (Beach Boy musical) having to perform in bikinis! It was amazing how quickly our self-pity turned into appreciation!".
- Jennie Ford

The parade will be done on a SAG-AFTRA contract because it is televised. The parade's committee will ask certain shows to perform. The show's producer will pay for their cast to perform, which is good advertising and bring in ticket sales. Once the producers and the creatives decide what number to perform, they will decide if they will include the swings or not. You will have a rehearsal at your own theatre. You will do a camera rehearsal on the street in front of Macy's. This will most likely be done on the street asphalt, as there is no time to set up and change sets for each Broadway show's performance and then dismantle before the parade crosses.

On the morning of the show, you will go for some parade rehearsal very early! It will be filmed outside no matter what; rain, snow, cold or sunny. You will get picked up at your home and then brought to a heated trailer outside of Macy's. You will wait your turn and rehearse with the cameras in costume. It is November in NYC, and it will most likely be chilly, possibly very chilly! There will be portable heaters blowing on the street to help, but be prepared with warm outerwear that you can shed easily before the cameras roll. You will likely have 2 different rehearsals outside, one in costume.

Broadway Softball League

"I love playing softball! I remember playing our first 'game' during SWEET SMELL OF SUCCESS. I was an outfielder and during the warm-up practise, I ran really hard to catch a fly ball that John Lithgow had nailed into the outfield. At the very last second, the sun blinded me as 'I swore' that ball was going into my glove. Nope! Right in the nose! Hard! I heard a crunch, saw my broken sunglasses fall to the ground, followed by uncontrollable drops of blood. John ran over to me with an extra T-shirt he had to stop the bleeding. My face swelled up and bruised. I had to call out of the show for 4 days because every time I tried to put my head down in the choreography, I felt like passing out. I was so embarrassed. Luckily, our producer was a softball fan and said I took one for the team! This is probably why some Creatives don't get excited about the Broadway softball season!" - Jennie Ford

In 1955, there was a formal softball league formed where cast, crew, producers and associates would play every summer Thursday afternoon in Central Park. It is now a 3 division, co-ed league played on the Heckscher Fields in Central Park every Thursday. It starts in the spring and may run as long as the end of August, if there are rain out days. The league is comprised of people who work on Broadway and Off-Broadway shows, union teams and theatrical organizations. The 11:30am division is usually for new shows because they frequently have Thursday afternoon rehearsals. The 1:30pm and the 3:30pm division include teams that have more of a history together. Some shows will join together to make one team if there is not enough interest from one company. It's a great theatrical community bonding experience while getting exercise and fresh air. At the end of each season, there is a party held with awards given out. You can also check out their website at www.broadwayshowleague.com for more information.

Broadway Bowling League

This league happens every Thursday night from midnight until 2:00am, currently at Port Authority's Leisure Time Bowling Alley (W.41st street at 8th Ave) in NYC. It is basically a non-competitive league. The idea is to have fun and raise money for BC/EFA. Each team pays a fee and then pays to bowl each week. This league happens periodically throughout the year on Thursday nights. At the end of each season, there is a party and an awards ceremony. For more information, check out their website at www.broadwaybowls.com.

The Gypsy Robe

This is a special ritual, dating back to 1950, only for chorus performers. Florence Baum was a chorus member in Gentlemen Prefer Blondes. She entered the men's dressing room wearing a pink robe with feathers. Each of the men took turns trying it on. Then one chorus member sent a robe to a friend performing in *Call Me Madame*. That show was a big success and so the robe was then sent to another chorus member of *Guys and Dolls* with a feathered rose attached from Ethel Merman's costume. The robe continued to be passed on from one show to another, each time with a memento added.

Since then, it has a more formal ritual with rules on how it's presented, who it's given to and how it's worn. It's given to the member of the chorus on opening night who has the most Broadway shows on a chorus contract. The company is gathered onstage before the opening night show. The previous winner of the robe stands onstage wearing the robe. This person would have received it on "opening night" of the previous Broadway musical. A short speech is given about the history, and then the robe is presented to the winner in the chorus. The winner puts on the robe. Everyone makes a big circle, and the winner walks counterclockwise in the circle three times as cast members reach out and touch the robe for good luck. Then that chorus member visits each dressing room while wearing the robe, to disperse good luck throughout the entire cast. Each show adds a memento to the robe. The chorus members sign it and pass it on to the next Broadway show's Gypsy winner. When the robe is full of mementos, it is returned and a new one is started. There is one on display in the Actor's Equity building in NYC.

Gypsy Of The Year

"Gypsy of the year" is an annual fundraising competition that runs for 6 weeks and includes Broadway, Off-Broadway, and national touring shows. Shows raise money for Broadway Cares/Equity Fights AIDS (BC/EFA). Each show that chooses to participate will make a curtain speech at the end of each show explaining the cause and ask for donations from the audience. The cast may also decide to sell signed playbills, signed posters, cast albums or anything to help raise money. Some companies have auctioned off a "meet and greet" with the show's star, or a piece of costume, a prop or an experience. At the end of 6 weeks, there is a show presented in a NY theatre called "Gypsy of the year". It is usually on a Monday night and Tuesday afternoon with the fundraising winners being announced on the last day. During the show, you will see outstanding performances and hilarious original skits. This show is usually a place to see the current Broadway stars as hosts or presenters. This event raises millions of dollars for BC/EFA each year.

Easter Bonnet

This is an annual fundraising competition for the Broadway, Off-Broadway and touring shows who wish to participate. The proceeds go to BC/EFA. In a period of 6 weeks the companies raise money by asking the audience for donations at curtain speeches, selling items, doing auctions and doing cabaret performances. At the end of the 6 weeks, there are two "Easter Bonnet" shows over two days with assorted skits, songs and dances, along with bonnets created specifically for the event. There are prizes awarded for the top fundraisers, the best presentation, and bonnet.

Broadway Bares

This is a burlesque fundraising show for BC/EFA, started by Broadway choreographer Jerry Mitchell in 1992. Broadway dancers, singers and actors perform striptease dances for the audience in NYC. This event usually happens over 2 shows and traditionally on Father's Day. It has since grown to more shows throughout the year. It combines the naughtiness of burlesque and the glitz and glamour of Broadway.

Broadway Barks

This is an annual animal adoption event that brings together many shelters and rescues in NYC. It started in 1999 and encourages animal adoption and educates people about being responsible owners. Celebrities like Bernadette Peters and Mary Tyler Moore host it, and many Broadway stars come and bring their pets.

Broadway Bears

This is a charity auction for BC/EFA where teddy bears are given custom costumes designed by a leading Broadway costume designer. The bears' outfits represent memorable characters from different plays or musicals and are given to the highest bidder.

The Broadway Flea Market

This is an annual flea market and grand auction that takes place in Shubert Alley each September. The theatre community and each theatre may put up a table to sell props, memorabilia, posters, costumes, or anything show-related to raise money for BC/EFA.

Carols For A Cure

This is a CD that is made annually by the contribution of different Broadway shows that want to participate. Each show gets to write something of its own to contribute to this holiday CD. It can be original or a remake of a familiar carol. The funds to make the CD are paid for by BC/EFA, and the proceeds for the sale of it go to BC/EFA. All the musicians, composers and singers donate their time.

CHAPTER 13

Saying Good Bye

There will come a time when the show closes or when you have to leave. It may be a positive or negative experience, depending on the circumstances.

The producers are evaluating weekly how their "investment" is doing. It is a business for them, and they have to make the hard decisions about when to cut their losses. It is negotiated in all of the union's contracts that they give a week's notice to close the show. That's it! No one wants a show to close prematurely. It's something that happens often though, and you should be prepared. Not every show is fortunate enough to have a long run with guaranteed tickets sales. You could come to work on Tuesday to find the closing notice posted on the callboard that your last show will be Sunday. Then it's back to auditioning and starting the whole process over again. This is something you get used to, and you have to be prepared for a career of uncertainty in theatre.

If you are the one who has to leave, you will have to give the company four weeks notice. This is done by giving management a "resignation letter". You can give it to the stage manager or company manager at work to indicate official notice you will be leaving.

The Broadway community is a small one. Once you are involved in it, you will likely see and work with many of the same people time and time again. It's a special place and everyone is supportive of each other and understands that "good bye" just means "until next time"!

Here is an example of a typical resignation letter:

Jennie Ford
555 W 46th street
New York, NY
10036
917-003-8930
jenford@gmail.com

June 9, 2013

EVITA
c/o Bespoke Theatricals
230 W.41st Street
New York, NY
10036

To Whom It May Concern:

Please accept this letter as my official notice that I will be leaving the show Sunday, July 7th. I have thoroughly enjoyed my time with EVITA and I will be sad to leave. I have been given an opportunity to perform a Principal role on another show. I will leave with such fond memories and great new friendships from this experience.

Thank you for the opportunities you have provided me during EVITA. Please let me know if I can be of any assistance during the transition with my replacement.

I will be forever grateful to have been part of this special show.

Sincerely,

Jennie Ford

You may have to give a resignation letter for some reason or another. You don't have to wait until the "4 week minimum notice to leave" before you hand in your letter. Extra notice is always appreciated so they can prepare to audition and train your replacement before you go.

You can unofficially let them know and wait to give official notice four weeks before leaving. There was an instance where an actor gave notice early, and then the show he was going to got cancelled. The replacement actor had signed a contract, so he was out of luck (and work).

Here is an example of a typical closing notice:

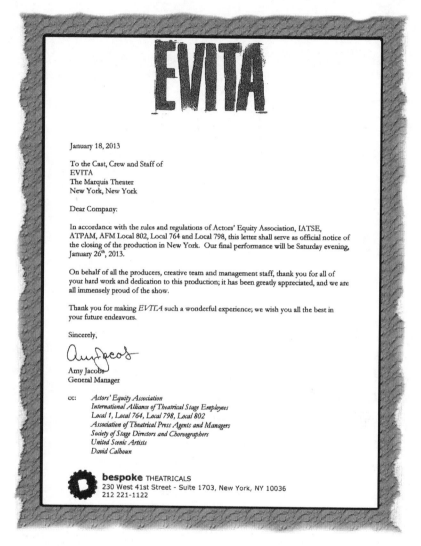

The closing notice may come as a surprise, or it may be anticipated. Either way, it's never easy for a general manager to post such a notice. They want to have every show run happily for years and years, make lots of money and provide thousands of jobs (including their own).

When the notice goes up, just make sure to take the time to thank all the people you have been working with. It means a lot to be acknowledged personally for the hard work you do. They may have been taken for granted, so a nice word goes a long way.

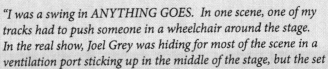

"I was a swing in ANYTHING GOES. In one scene, one of my tracks had to push someone in a wheelchair around the stage. In the real show, Joel Grey was hiding for most of the scene in a ventilation port sticking up in the middle of the stage, but the set piece was never there in rehearsal each week. In an effort to be authentic, too, they found an antique wheelchair that was extremely difficult to steer, especially with someone in it! I tried to practice pushing Linda around the stage, but nothing could really prepare me for the real scene, where there were many more people and set pieces. Every time I went on, I think I ran Linda in to about five set pieces by the time I could get her offstage. It was so embarrassing! And that ventilation pipe was my worst nightmare. It was big, center stage, and holding an Oscar winner! There were times when I came within an inch of knocking it over!" - Margot De La Barre

"I pride myself on not being easily rattled, but one show at THE MUSIC MAN pushed me to my limits. I covered 10 girls in the show. Then it was decided that I should cover another 3 boys as a second cover because the other male swing was a 6 foot tall man and was covering boys of 11-16 years of age. One day I got thrown on for one of those boys. I had no costumes for that track and it hadn't really been planned out in each department as to what would actually happen if I went on. I was cramming the information of this foreign track into my head while each department was vying for my time. It was very stressful. The costume department ended up putting me in his costume which was boy knickers, suspenders, shirt and tie. Then the hair department just French-Braided my hair close to my head so I didn't stand out as a girl. I had to dance center stage with all the boys, do a cartwheel off a table, lift Marion the Librarian along with two other boys, and partner and lift a little 9 year old girl. I laid on my dressing room floor and started crying as I vented. I felt like the androgynous one that everyone in the audience would be laughing at. I didn't even know who I was in the play, let alone them being okay with paying over $100 per ticket to see me! The show went well but I hoped it would never happen again." - Jennie Ford

CHAPTER 14

How To Create Your Swing Books

There are many ways to create a system to facilitate your job as a swing. There is no right or wrong way; it just comes down to personal preference. One system may work for you, but not as well for others. This chapter is about giving yourself the tools to make you the most effective swing you can be. (This chapter will use emphasize many of the tips and learning techniques covered previously in Chapter 7.)

Start with broad strokes, while getting as many details as you can! Write *everything* down, such as staging, choreography, director's intentions, vocal notes, props, entrances and exits. Scribble notes in your margins or on the back of your pages to help you later. Don't worry about how messy it is; just write, write, write! You can pull out the information needed, as it pertains to each of your actors, to create a more manageable system. Your final system will become your "go-to" guide that you use on a daily basis.

Here are the three steps to create a system for yourself:

1) **Start Broad: Write down Everything for Everyone.**
2) **Make a "Rough" Tracking System for Each Actor you cover.**
3) **Make a "Permanent" Tracking System for Each Actor you cover.**

1) Start Broad: Write down Everything for Everyone.

Write down the staging

Once the choreographer starts to stage, just get the overall information down in one large book. Grab a sharp pencil, a good eraser and lots of paper. The paper can be lined, blank or stage graphs of the number you are working on.

Include any special things the choreographer or director say. It could be numbers they want actors to be on, props they hold, intentions, words to move on, or anything else they deem as important.

Here's an example of **staging, using lined paper**: (The "built-in" lines are helpful for placing actors in the same line for any production number.)

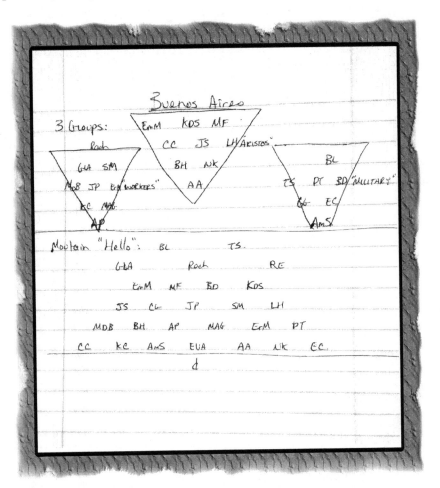

Here's an example of **staging, using a blank piece of paper**: (It's great because it gives you lots of room for notes. You may have to write in more information than you would if you used blank stage graphs.)

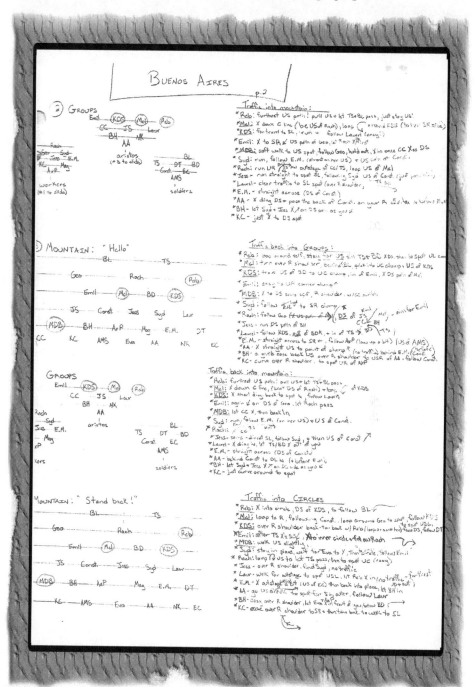

Here's an example of **staging, using a stage chart**: (It is useful to quickly chart where an actor goes. You can see the numbers, tracks, and wings.)

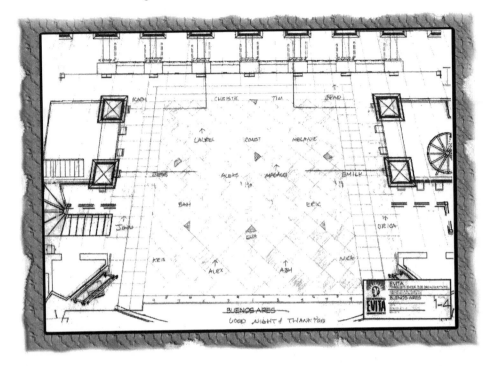

TIP:

There will be some time during rehearsal when the creative team will be working on a section you are not involved in. Use that time to go over your charts. Clean them up, so you understand them. Ask other swings or the dance captain if you have any questions, such as numbers the actors were placed on. Then, get yourself ready for the next scheduled production number you are involved in.

Write down the choreography

Write down the choreography as you learn it, otherwise you are likely to forget. You will learn multiple numbers in a short period of time. It's impossible to remember all the essential details, so use writing as a tool to help you remember. Write it directly onto your music or on a blank piece of paper.

Here's an example of writing the **choreography directly onto your music**.

Here's an example of writing the **choreography on a blank piece of paper**.

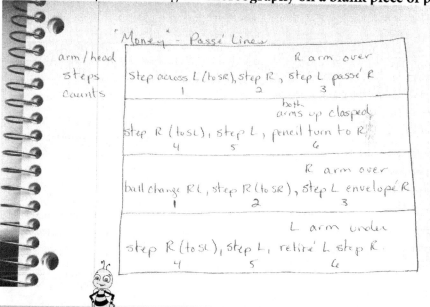

TIP:

You can also video tape yourself using specific notes such as "remember your head is downstage on count 1". When you review it, you will have the information you need. If you aren't a competent dancer, then you may ask the dance captain if you can video him/her dancing when he/she has time. It's not their job, but they are usually happy to help you!

2) Make a Rough Tracking System for Each Actor

Now that you have the picture of the show "as a whole", you can break the information down in more detail for each actor you cover. This is a temporary system to let you manage anything if you were to be "thrown on". If it's a new show, there will be many changes before opening night, but you still need a system before opening. To do this, you make "rough" individual tracking sheets, as needed. These won't have all the specific details of each track, but at least you can get by without hurting anyone and can maintain your pride along the way. It should include important information like props, entrances and exits, any dancing or singing features, partners, and so forth.

Here's an example of a **"rough" tracking sheet, hand-written**. It can be done quickly, to get through a day where you have to step in for someone.

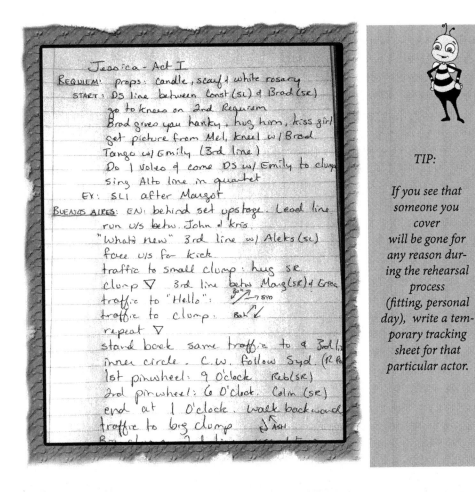

TIP:

If you see that someone you cover will be gone for any reason during the rehearsal process (fitting, personal day), write a temporary tracking sheet for that particular actor.

Here's an example of a **"rough" tracking sheet, done on the computer.** If you do it on a computer, you can easily update it as changes are made to the show. It helps to date it, so you know if it is the most recent version.

EVITA: ALEKS PEVEC

DRESS SL HALLWAY FOR TOP OF SHOW

ACT I
REQUIEM
Start in 2nd line between BD and MF w/ candle and cross (cross in jacket pocket)
Finish in most US line
Lift both arms on 5th "Evita" as lines arrive, and bring arms down before 2nd Req

OH WHAT A CIRCUS
Stay standing in spot for most of song
Turn to face US on "Pretty bad state for a state to be in' & BH will come to you
Hug BH on "one who's died"
Mourning tango w/ BH in 3rd line SL2
Do bolero x4 (cheat DS after 2nd boleo)
Exit out stage SL catacomb

COSTUME CHANGE INTO WORKER IN SL HALLWAY

BUENOS AIRES
Follow LH for entrance snake.
Follow CG US to be opposite MAGALDI in window of BH & EVA
Face US 1st time
Walk DSR diagonal into SR triangle, keeping US of AS
DS point of triangle
Follow MAGALDI to "mountain" position
2nd in window between AS & EVA for "Mountain"
Turn back on self to loop around MAGALDI and follow him into DSR triangle
DS point of triangle
Follow MAGALDI to mountain position
Walk on spot to get in position for circle
3rd circle going clockwise following MD
1st link: 7 o'clock with LH and BL
2nd link: 1 o'clock with KC and RE
Pinwheel: at 9 o'clock
Walk DS and loop back in to be in front line between KC and M for workers speech
Follow RP to travel to US of group
Stand on outside of KDS R shoulder for military speech
Follow KDS to travel to middle of group
Stand behind KDS for aristo speech
Follow NK DS to loop around EVA for partnering break finishing SR on DS of NK
1st eight in place
Cross SL to be US of CG by overhead lift
Walk SR towards center by the time JS starts partnering
Have moment w/ MAGALDI
Partner SR side of EVA for trio w/ NK
SL side of EVA for six men w/ EVA
L side of T lift grabbing shoulder and arm
Travel DS to 1st line between EVA and ER for lunges, starting L foot first
Follow ER for snake
Travel straight DS for button

BUENOS AIRES PLAYOFF
Partner EVA for play off and exit USL w/ her for Lovers

GOOD NIGHT AND THANK YOU
Get kimono offstage at top of spiral stairs and walk US to inside of apartment
Close door behind EVA as she steps out on balcony

3) Make a Permanent Tracking System for Each Actor

Once the show is close to opening, the show gets "frozen". Once a show is frozen, you can make a permanent tracking system. It's best to wait until the show is frozen to eliminate unnecessary work, to keep your notes up to date and accurate. The attention to detail in your permanent tracking sheets is going to separate you from being a good swing to being an extraordinary swing! This becomes your "life-line" of answers you need. The more specifics you have in your system, the better. No brain could handle all the minutiae of an entire show for every actor!

Here's an example of a **temporary chart**: (It was a first draft chart, done before getting on the stage, so the positions are more vague than the final version.)

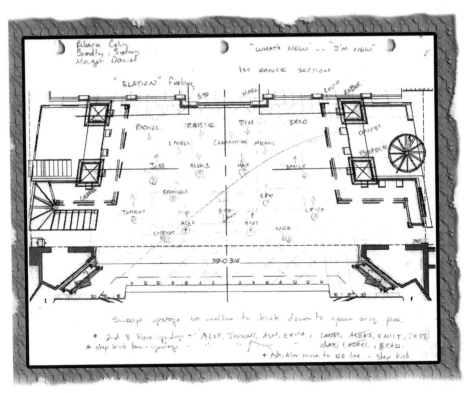

You will find big changes between your temporary tracking and your permanent one. There are many changes once you get onto the actual stage. There may be more markings you can use as references, such as wings or tracks you didn't have before. Once you get on the stage, you may find the front edge of the stage has a 6 foot drop to the audience's seats. Many actors are not comfortable standing as close to the edge where they may have been blocked in the studio. Many of these elements change when you move from the studio to the stage, but they will ultimately help you with your specificity and details.

Here's an example of a **permanent chart**:

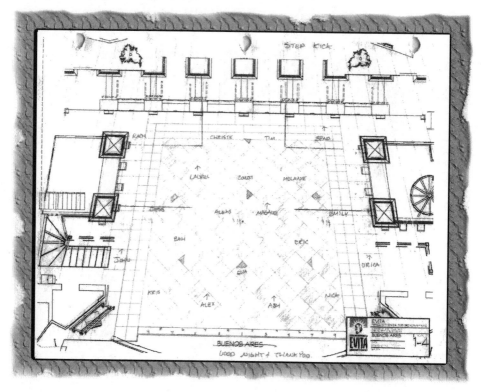

Once the cast was onstage, there were "diamond" markings and speakers on the stage floor that helped with placing the actors *very* specifically.

These charts are written from the perspective of the audience because that is where this swing learned the positions. She also watched the show from this point of view, so she chose to write it like this. You can also switch the graphs 180 degrees and write it from the actor's point of view. There is no right or wrong way, and there are benefits to both. It depends on how you process information. For some swings, it may be easier to write it from the actor's point of view, making it easy to review onstage before you go on.

It's very helpful to make a system that you can quickly and easily access individual actors' tracks. If you get thrown on during a show, it is much easier when you don't have to sift through 26 people to find the information you need. If you tend to process more quickly looking at pictures and diagrams rather than reading, here are some suggestions:

Coiled index tracking books

You can make individual books for each of the actors you cover with mini ground plans. The mini ground plans would only contain information that is pertinent to that actor.

You can keep your original graphs, charts and information in a big binder for reference and just use the individual tracking sheets on a day-to-day basis.

In order to make the coiled index books, you need to create some mini ground plans, cut them and glue them. It becomes a bit of an "arts and crafts" project. It's trial and error, to get the size you want and yet leave room on the pages for notes.

The "4x6" coiled index books are a good size for carrying around backstage. They are small and accessible. They don't rely on battery power. The only downside is they cannot be emailed to yourself! Electronic versions are nice to have incase you are called at home notifying you that you will be on. Portable, electronic systems allow you to have your tracks with you at all times. They can give you more time to look at the information on your way to the theatre.

Inside each book, you would have a quick reference to the information you need for that one actor's track. The details of each track make you stand out as an extraordinary swing. Write more than you think you'll need in your individual books. You may not feel it's necessary now, but once you do 5 different tracks in the same week, you will find it useful to have every bit of information written down. This helps avoid mistakes and puts you on top of your game. No matter how well you know a track, it can get confusing if you haven't done it in a while or have had to do other tracks recently. The little details start to meld together.

A good thing to include is "pre-show" information. Use the first page to write down your wig time and with whom. Where do you change into your clothes and with whom? Where do you get your mic? What are your props for the top of the show, and where do you get them? What are you wearing for this particular track? What vocal line do you sing.

You can include a "wish list" you would like to do before the show, if given the time. This could include things like partnering with people, touching scenery, rehearsing a quick change or asking the dance captain to run through any difficult traffic with the company.

You can write difficult traffic you need, making sure no one gets hurt. Traffic is notated with arrows. The person who goes first has a solid arrow. The person who has to wait has a "gap" in the arrow. You can also include everything specific to that track, such as hand grips for partnering, choreography reminders, and vocal reminders.

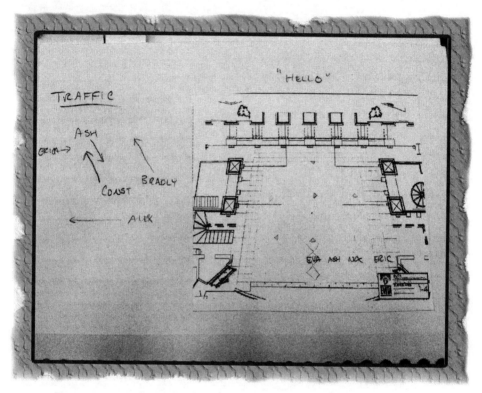

Between numbers, look at your onstage business and your costume, mic and wig changes backstage to know where you go and when. The show is as much choreographed offstage as it is onstage.

It's also important to know how much time you have to look at your books during the show. There may be three numbers back-to-back so you don't have time to look at your notes. It's good to indicate those moments somehow, so you know when you have to look ahead.

In the example on the next page, you see the number clearly stated as "Requiem". The notes tell you specifically what props to use, who to stand between, when to move, who to interact with, what physical action to take and where to return your props.

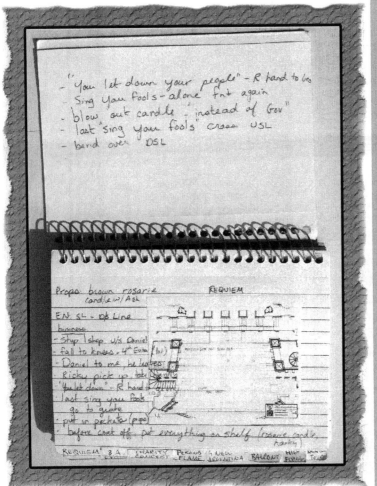

In this example, the swing placed sticky tabs in her book to indicate where she could look at her book during the show. She knew she had to review all the information from one tab to the next. Time is extremely valuable! 10 extra seconds will buy you another 5-7 pieces of valuable information.

Computerized tracking sheets

Another way of constructing swing books is to have computerized tracking sheets for each actor. They can be done by hand or by computer so they are easily accessible from anywhere.

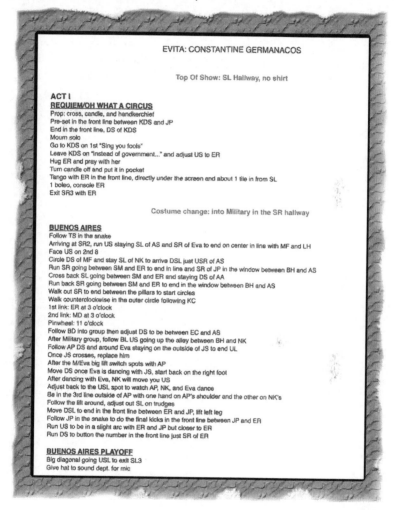

EVITA: CONSTANTINE GERMANACOS

Top Of Show: SL Hallway, no shirt

ACT I
REQUIEM/OH WHAT A CIRCUS
Prop: cross, candle, and handkerchief
Pre-set in the front line between KDS and JP
End in the front line, DS of KDS
Mourn solo
Go to KDS on 1st "Sing you fools"
Leave KDS on "instead of government..." and adjust US to ER
Hug ER and pray with her
Turn candle off and put it in pocket
Tango with ER in the front line, directly under the screen and about 1 tile in from SL
1 boleo, console ER
Exit SR3 with ER

Costume change: into Military in the SR hallway

BUENOS AIRES
Follow TS in the snake
Arriving at SR2, run US staying SL of AS and SR of Eva to end on center in line with MF and LH
Face US on 2nd 8
Circle DS of MF and stay SL of NK to arrive DSL just USR of AS
Run SR going between SM and ER to end in line and SR of JP in the window between BH and AS
Cross back SL going between SM and ER and staying DS of AA
Run back SR to end in the window between BH and AS
Walk out SR to end between the pillars to start circles
Walk counterclockwise in the outer circle following KC
1st link: ER at 3 o'clock
2nd link: MD at 3 o'clock
Pinwheel: 11 o'clock
Follow BD into group then adjust DS to be between EC and AS
After Military group, follow BL US going up the alley between BH and NK
Follow AP DS and around Eva staying on the outside of JS to end UL
Once JS crosses, replace him
After the M/Eva big lift switch spots with AP
Move DS once Eva is dancing with JS, start back on the right foot
After dancing with Eva, NK will move you US
Adjust back to the USL spot to watch AP, NK, and Eva dance
Be in the 3rd line outside of AP with one hand on AP's shoulder and the other on NK's
Follow the lift around, adjust out SL on trudges
Move DSL to end in the front line between ER and JP, lift leg
Follow JP in the snake to do the final kicks in the front line between JP and ER
Run US to be in a slight arc with ER and JP but closer to ER
Run DS to button the number in the front line just SR of ER

BUENOS AIRES PLAYOFF
Big diagonal going USL to exit SL3
Give hat to sound dept. for mic

This system is quick and easy to do. Once you are finished, you can place all the tracking sheets into one binder and separate each actor's track with tabs. When you get called to go on, just remove your pages from the binder and put them back in when the show is over. Computerizing it gives you the advantage of accessibility and flexibility to change as you go. The only disadvantage is you have to read everything. If you write many details, it could take a long time to get the information. You need this information quickly during the show.

Combination tracking sheets

Some people can absorb information faster by looking at graphs and pictures versus reading. One swing found a way to combine both computerized and picture tracking sheets. She would input the stage picture on the computer so she had a quick reference of where she should be, without having to read every detail.

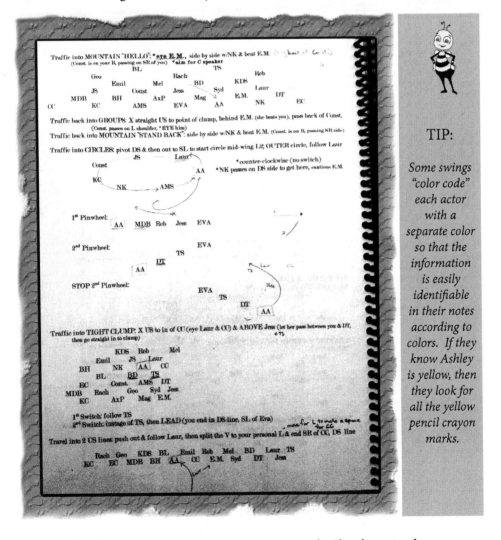

All of her track sheets were computerized. She drew in the positions of where people were in the formations and wrote the traffic in by hand. She found once she did the work to create one picture, she could cut and paste it into every track sheet so she wouldn't have to do it over and over for each actor.

Once she was finished making all of her tracking sheets, she took everything to an office supply store and had the pages bound into one book. Her book included all her tracking sheets, along with her original rehearsal charts, notes, traffic patterns, and choreography.

Each track was labeled, so she could easily flip to anyone's track needed at the time. She appreciated the coiled book so she could flip the pages easily and was not as cumbersome as a huge binder. The pages would fold over onto themselves and fit easily on her lap backstage. She also liked having all her original rehearsal notes and graphs incase she had a question while she was looking at a specific actor's track.

As she went on more for each track, she became comfortable to the point where she didn't need her big book anymore. Each track was in her computer, so she could print off one track to carry around during a show. It meant that she only needed a few pages of papers stapled together rather than her larger book.

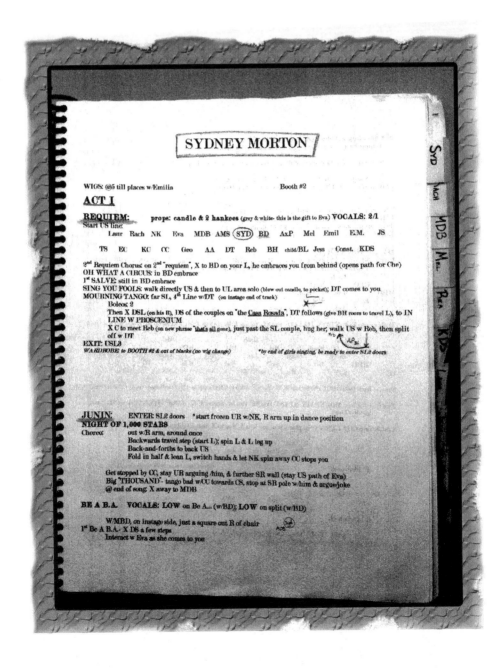

Comprehensive, "broad-stroke" notes may be too much to read when you are on for one track. It's important to make individual tracking notes to save time. She used her comprehensive notes to create notes for individual tracks. She used individual tracks to assist her when performing. If she found she was missing details in her individual tracks, she would refer back to her original notes in her big book and add them to her individual tracks for future.

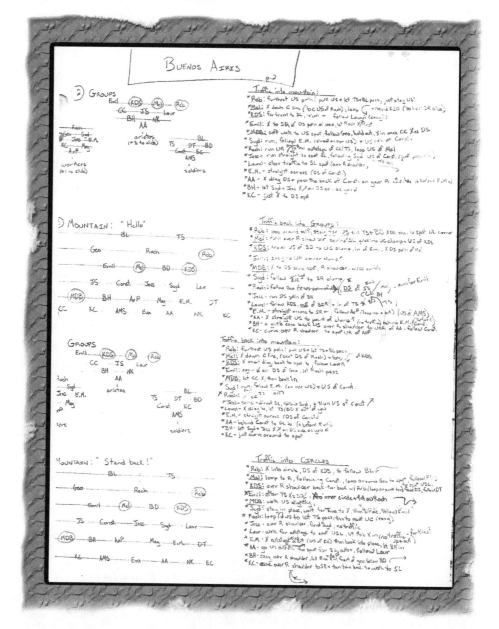

Messy to Marvelous

No matter what your method is, expect it will go through a process to get it to where you want. The final product will look marvelous, but the originals will seem messy. Don't get too hung up on the look in the beginning. Just concentrate on gathering as much information as you can, quickly.

To the right you see an example of a temporary, first draft chart versus the permanent, final chart below it. The original chart contains much detailed information that the final chart does not.

This original chart is from EVITA. It was the moment after Juan Peron is elected and everyone had gathered to see and cheer him on. It was the moment before Eva's famous song on the balcony "Don't cry for me Argentina". The original chart has everything written from what the director said, to who is holding hankies. Some important information from this chart is:

- The director told the cast they are seeing the "newly elected" Juan Peron, for the first time.
- It was choreographed that the curtain would go up while everyone cheered and spread out, to fill the stage once the curtain was out.
- The cast was told to bring their vocal shouts down when Che started to speak.
- The cast was told to make their bodies face directly upstage, yet take their focus to the center of the balcony. This made the stage look more full than if everyone's bodies were also facing towards center.
- The cast was facing upstage away from the conductor and couldn't see the monitor. Johnny was made the onstage conductor for cut off's.
- Everyone was told to shake their hankies on the last "Evita" until the music stopped.
- Everyone had to bring two hankies onstage (used one and hid one) except for the maids, who exited during the number. When the maids exited, everyone would wave their second hanky to make it look like there were still the same amount of people onstage.

You can put this information somewhere else so the final chart is not so "crowded". Then draw a line through the original chart so you know it's not the most recent one you are referencing.

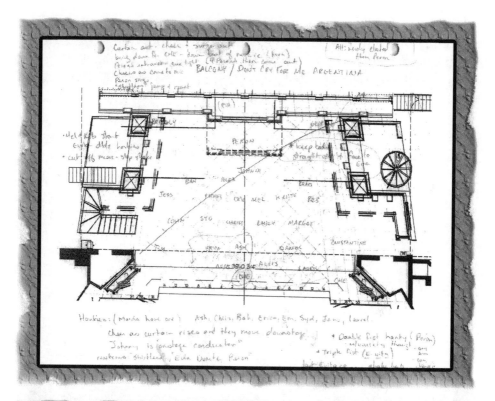

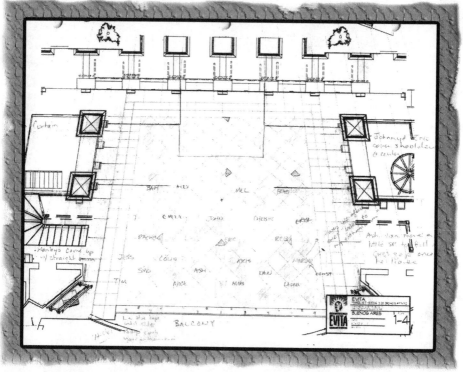

Here is an example of the choreography quickly handwritten and then computerized with more detail, for a swing binder. It doesn't need to be pretty, it just needs to gather information you will need later. From this, you can tell the music is counted in 3's (123, 123). "Water" is a term that the choreographer used for a step he created.

Here is an example of the choreography, cleaned up and clarified, for a swing's permanent book. It is more specific as to what choreography is happening on what count of the music. It was created using a table in microsoft word. The left column has the counts of the music. The second column contains the lyrics of the song. The third column has the choreography that relates to the music at that time.

MONEY
(Guy's Choreography for Dance Break)

1-3 1-3		GUYS: "Water" step to L (1) to SL, end with R foot behind (3), Step RL (12) to SR, flick kick R (3)
1-3 1-3		GUYS: "Water" step facing upstage L (1) to SR, end R foot behind and face front (3), ball change back R (1), LR (23)
1-3 1-3		GUYS: Jump up (1) off R foot with L leg out to 90 degrees (arms up) then envelope in and land on R and present arms to her R over L (3). Lift the girl off the ground and tilt arms to SL for her fan (3)
1-3 1-3		GUYS: Step R (1) to SL, drag L (2) turning to R while still holding girl's R hand, step L foot together (3). Ball change back R (1), step L (2) and grab girl for sit lift. R hand around her R knee and inner thigh. L hand under and around butt. She will bring her L leg up to other.
1-3 1-3		GUYS: Lift girl and turn her to your left (CCW)..123, put her down SL of you 123. (2 turns)
1-3 1-3 1-3	*(Thank God for Switzerland music)*	GUYS: Spin to the left with arms out and head up. Do as many rotations as you can with feet out of time to music.
1-3 1-3		GUYS: Step out LRL (123) to SL (turning to the left) arms out-up-out and head to SL, "Water" Step R drag L (facing front) with arms free and moving up body with head free and moving up.
1-3 1-3		GUYS: Step out LRL (&123) facing upstage this time and use catch step (ball change) to get into it. Face front and do ball change back R(1), LR (23)
1-3 1-3		GUYS: Forward roll (L shoulder to R hip) (12), then stand up on L foot and pivot U/S to face girl (3). Step LRL (to meet girl) and let her fan kick (3) while you face U/S
1-3 1-3		GUYS: Step LR (12), fan kick L (3) facing the front. Step L plant R (12) to spin around and face the front and dip girl (3)
1-3 1-3		GUYS: Bring the girl up (1), step out L (2) to SL, bring R foot into L (2) with arms up, step out L (3) to SL with arms out. Step out L (1) to SL and arms out, bring R foot to L (2) while grabbing girls torso with L arm and bringing her to you. Step out lunge L (3) to SL while grabbing girl's L hamstring above her knee.
1-3		GUYS: Bring girl up onto her leg (1), step L (2) while switching arm grip, step out lunge R (3) while grabbing girl's R ankle.

Here is an example of a track sheet before it is finalized for a swing binder. The swing prints off the temporary, draft version and then adds more detailed notes when they "trail" or go on for the actor. Again, the more information, the better. Here the swing added backstage notes, traffic notes and tips to help him be more specific.

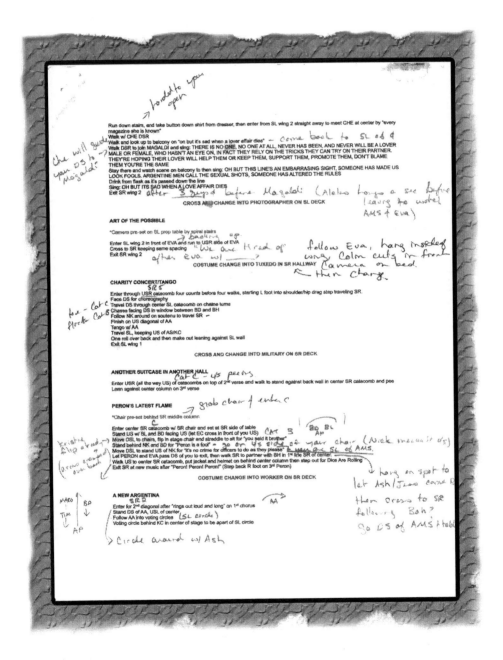

Here is an example of the same track sheet, after it's been cleaned up. The swing incorporated all the notes added in pencil to his original. He kept these permanent tracking sheets in a binder and pulled them out every time he went on for a specific track.

Run down stairs, and take button down shirt (dresser hands it to you as you come down the stairs) then enter from SL2 straight away to meet CHE at center by "every magazine she is known"
Put shirt on during Che's solo
Che will guide you DSR on "...but we don't always answer..."
Walk back to SL of center and look up to balcony on "on but it's sad when a love affair dies..."
Walk DSR to join MAGALDI

Vocal: "THERE IS NO ONE, NO ONE AT ALL, NEVER HAS BEEN, AND NEVER WILL BE A LOVER MALE OR FEMALE, WHO HASN'T AN EYE ON, IN FACT THEY RELY ON THE TRICKS THEY CAN TRY ON THEIR PARTNER. THEY'RE HOPING THEIR LOVER WILL HELP THEM OR KEEP THEM, SUPPORT THEM, PROMOTE THEM, DON'T BLAME THEM YOU'RE THE SAME"

Stay there and watch scene on balcony to then sing: "OH BUT THIS LINE'S AN EMBARRASSING SIGHT, SOMEONE HAS MADE US LOOK FOOLS. ARGENTINE MEN CALL THE SEXUAL SHOTS, SOMEONE HAS ALTERED THE RULES"
Drink from flask as it's passed down the line
Sing: "OH BUT ITS SAD WHEN A LOVE AFFAIR DIES"
Exit SR2 following CC (Hang out for a second to watch Eva and Alex before exiting)

CROSS AND CHANGE INTO PHOTOGRAPHER ON SL DECK

ART OF THE POSSIBLE
*Camera pre-set on SL prop table by spiral stairs
Enter SL2 in front of EVA (backing up) and run to USR side of EVA
Cross to SR ("We are tired of") keeping same spacing
Exit SR2 (follow Eva, hang inside of wing, Colin cuts in front then place camera on the bed on your way to QC.

COSTUME CHANGE INTO TUXEDO IN SR HALLWAY

CHARITY CONCERT/TANGO
Enter through USR5 catacomb four counts before four walks, starting L foot into shoulder/hip drag step traveling SR.
Face DS for choreography
Travel DS through catacomb C on chaine turns (toe touch happens in catacomb B)
Chasse facing DS in window between BD and BH
Follow NK around on soutenu to travel SR
Finish on USL diagonal of AA
Tango w/ AA
Travel SL, keeping US of AS/KC
One roll over back and then make out leaning against SL wall
Exit SL wing 1

CROSS AND CHANGE INTO MILITARY ON SR DECK

ANOTHER SUITCASE IN ANOTHER HALL
Enter USR (all the way US) of catacombs on top of 2nd verse & walk to stand against back wall in catacomb C to pee
Lean against center column on 3rd verse

PERON'S LATEST FLAME
*Chair pre-set behind SR middle column
Enter catacomb C w/ SR chair and set at SR side of table
Stand US in catacomb B w/ BL and BD facing US (let EC cross in front of you US   BD   BL   AP
Move DSL to chairs and straddle to sit for "you said it brother" (arms folded across chair back)
Stand behind NK and BD for "Peron is a fool" (be on US side of your chair just SL of AMS)
Follow BD DSL to end standing SR of BD for "it's no crime for officers to do as they please"
Let PERON and EVA pass DS of you to exit. Hang on the spot to let AA and JP come DS, then cross to SR following BH (stay DS of AMS and the table) to partner with BH in 1st line SR of center.
Walk US to catacomb C (SR of BD and SL of TS and MDB), put jacket and helmet on behind center column then step out SR for Dice Are Rolling
Exit SR at new music after "Peron! Peron! Peron!" (Step back R foot on 3rd Peron)

COSTUME CHANGE INTO WORKER ON SR DECK

Even though this is a "permanent system", be open to change. There are times when "brush up" rehearsals happen and minor things change that were perhaps missed in the haste of getting the show up. Traffic may be altered to help make it easier, and it could change whether you go upstage or downstage of someone. There will be things you learn and add along the way. An actor might find they would benefit from changing the way they did something before, and you will need to change it in all your books.

There are numerous ways to come up with a system for swinging. You will forever be perfecting your system as you go from job to job and learn what works best for you. Don't get overwhelmed or be too hard on yourself if you don't know what works for you yet.

The details are what makes you stand out. You will gain so much respect if you go onstage and have noted that "this girl" likes the hand grip a particular way. You will get kudos if you do the same staged business as the actor you are replacing, even though it wasn't choreographed or given by the director. You will be applauded after every show if you know whether you go upstage or downstage of another actor during the dance transitions. You will be respected by the crew if you know where to change your costumes and where to pick up your props. Your reputation precedes you more than you know. This business is small and every choreographer, stage manager, dance captain, dresser, wig person and prop man will work in many shows after this one. You want to be the person who everyone talks about in a positive way. This will help build your career in this business and not just this show for right now.

The last thing you want is for people to feel they have to take care of you during your show. Show them you are in charge and know what you are doing. They will be more confident and not worry about you. Even if you feel overwhelmed, try not to voice it or show it a lot. Pick one or two people that you can confide in, preferably not in the show. Let your frustrations out elsewhere as you maneuver your way through this "swing" contract.

Protect your future career by keeping the emotions out of your workplace. Yes! It's hard! Broadway is hard! When you are stressed, you are in a different reality than many people around you. They won't be able to understand what you are going through until they have to go through it themselves. You can turn your attitude around by speaking positively, smiling and making the most out of this "harried" experience! What's truly the worst that could happen? If it's not death, then it's probably not that big a deal!

"WEST SIDE STORY. So, Broadway Debut. Originally hired as a Jet swing/assistant dance captain. Somewhere along the way between our out of town tryout in Washington D.C. and opening night on Broadway, the creative team made the decision that I would also be a secondary Shark swing in anticipation for the days we would start experiencing crazy split-track shows.

I personally feel like the first few months of a new production are the hardest (and also most exciting) for a swing. Changes are constantly being made and until the show is frozen a week or so before opening night, we have to learn to stay flexible and prioritize the information we get to be most productive. In my case, that meant prioritizing the Jet boy tracks.

A couple of weeks after we opened, I got the call from my stage manager on Saturday morning to tell me I would be going on for one of the Sharks at the 2pm matinee. Ha! Surely not already? I was also aware that our director, Arthur Laurents planned to attend the matinee. For the most part, the show was fine. The most entertaining part for the rest of the cast was seeing what my Shark costumes looked like.

I did my homework prior to going on, but I did have one epic disaster of a fall right at the top of the show. I had managed to make it through most of the Prologue, and we were coming up to ear piercing moment with A-Rab. Basically we corner him, he runs and jumps into the shark boys and flips over before we drag him on his back downstage. I was responsible for holding one of his arms and facilitating the flip. I was also one of the boys responsible for dragging him downstage. I still can't tell you what happened, but one moment A-Rab was flipping in the air, then the next thing I know, I was on the ground next to A-Rab, still holding his arm, being dragged downstage along with A-Rab. You could have fried an egg on my face. I think Pepe pulled me up to my feet. In all honesty, it was such a quick moment, but it felt like forever for me. The only thing that went through my mind was 'Arthur Laurents is here, and I just had a blowout'."
- Michaeljon Slinger

"I remember the day when I decided that I shouldn't be a swing anymore. There is a certain temperament needed to be a swing, and although I thought of myself as a great swing, I said something one day that made me realize that maybe my temperament wasn't the best fit for swinging anymore. I was the dance captain and the swing on the show, so I had the duty of giving people notes at the same time as covering them. This can sometimes be a tricky situation. Some of the guys seemed somewhat territorial over their spacing and came across as insecure or guarded when I gave them a note. One guy gave me a lot of flack and I just got frustrated and said, 'Okay. Just don't get sick! You won't want to be out of the show when the creatives come because if they see me do your part, you may be out of a job!'. I knew right then I shouldn't swing anymore. Being good at your job as a swing is only half of it. The other half is how you handle people and personalities and all stuff that comes along with it". - Dennis Stowe

"I always knew I loved to swing, but I never thought about why until the day my mother came to see me in my first Broadway show, Mamma Mia! As she was walking me to the theater I got a call from Stage Management saying that instead of the track I was scheduled to go on for, there was going to be a cut show. I was going to go on for 3 different parts, one of them a male track that was not part of my normal responsibilities. My mother later told me how stressed she was watching that performance and how by the end of Act 1 she was sweating because she was so nervous for me. She said she didn't think she exhaled until the curtain call. I remember that day differently. I remember loving getting that call and feeling energized and excited as we tried to figure out the cut show. I knew that days like those would put my hard work as a swing to the test, and I welcomed the challenge of putting my cast members at ease in a show with so many people missing.

Hearing my mother's story made me realize that I loved to swing because last minute changes didn't stress me out. Had that call from Stage Management caused anxiety, I would have had a difficult time retaining the information I needed. Instead of two hours of "I can't wait until this is over" I found the last minute changes to be exciting and energizing. I did the job I was hired to do, had fun in the process and was confident that I helped make the show run smoothly. - Rachel Bress

CHAPTER 15

What Broadway people say makes the Best Swing

I decided to do a little experiment of my own and survey the Broadway community to determine what they believed were the most important traits for being the best swing. I had an overwhelming response from over 60 Broadway professionals. They came from directors, dressers, current and past swings. There were people who hadn't swung personally but knew what it was like to be in a show with good and not so good swings.

Some words and phrases that were repeatedly used to describe the best swings:

Ability to stay calm under pressure
Organized and prepared
Detail oriented
Having a good attitude
Being a team player
Flexible with change
Focused
Adaptable
Versatile
Quick thinkers
Multi-taskers
Confident, but not arrogant

Willing to take risks and put themselves out there
Personality that's easy to get along with
Good temperament for the job
The most talented person in the cast
The ones with the broadest training
Not easily offended
Low maintenance
Good sense of humor
Courteous chameleons
Cool as a cucumber at all times; astronaut-like
Always have the big picture in mind
Have to know every brush stroke of the painting
Brings fresh energy on stage, but blends in seamlessly

Some valuable observations

"You have to have both the brain and the personality for the job. Some of it can be learned and some is inherent, but you need both qualities." - Michael McGurk (*The Music Man, The Wedding Singer, A Tree Grows in Brooklyn*)

"It has a lot to do with the person swinging. The good ones are usually the Type A's, but also can be laid back...the over-achievers, but can take it if they screw up. They see the big picture, but can blend. They don't get bent out of shape when something crazy happens, like split-tracks or going on for the opposite gender. I think the good ones also like it, even when they are complaining about what they are doing. Swinging is hard.. But it's also a lot of fun." - Callie Carter (*Elf-The Musical, Monty Python's Spamalot, Evita, 42nd Street*)

"Someone who can adapt well when he/she is out of their comfort zone. Go with the flow, stay calm under pressure and let go a little of the perfectionist side of yourself. I learned that things won't always go as I practised, rehearsed or 'swear I saw'. If I made a mistake, I would make a note of it and it wouldn't happen twice. That made the other cast members trust me more." - Rachel Bress (*9 to 5: The Musical, People In The Picture, The Pirate Queen, Mamma Mia, Wicked, West Side Story*)

"You must continue to mentally 'turn the page' as you perform; don't expend any energy thinking about what just happened, be it bad or good. Keep yourself physically in the moment and mentally just one step ahead...but only one step. If you think too far in advance, you will mess up what you are doing in the moment. After the show is over, then you can assess what you have learned and make notes for the next time. Make the corrections immediately in your notes because that's when they are the most fresh, clear, and accurate in your head." - Paul Castree *(The Scarlet Pimpernel, High Fidelity, Grease, All Shook Up, Footloose, Saturday Night Fever, Dreamgirls, Funny Girl, Movin' Out, Hair, Young Frankenstein, 9 to 5: The Musical, The Most Happy Fella)*

"It was so amazing to see the same show from 10 different perspectives. I loved stealing everyone's good bits and making them my own. I learned the most about myself as an actor while swinging." - Ryan Wilson *(Nation Tours: Hairspray, Wizard of Oz)*

"I love and respect swings who ask the right questions and stay on top of changes that are constantly being made during the run of the show. I love when a swing respects the work (blocking, choreography, beats) of the person they are covering so it is seamless for the rest of the cast too." Charlo Crossley *(The Color Purple, Hairspray, Tricks, Jesus Christ Superstar, Bette Midler's Clams on the Half Shell Review)*

"I have been in a long-running show with a lot of swings who have been there for a while. In that show, the swings go on way more than other shows. The best swings are the ones who don't complain when they get called to go on." - Anonymous

"Do you want to be right or happy? Swings generally know the show better than the onstage cast because they stand next to the dance supervisors and 'creatives' during clean up rehearsals. However, it's really important to understand that a show can morph and change into what happens on stage every night. For instance, an actor may have been told to enter in wing 3, but it slowly changes to wing 2 as the months go by. As a swing, you want to do the correct blocking, but if you came out in wing 3, everyone would think you didn't know what you were doing. You have to find the balance of being right and the flexibility to adapt to what's being done currently." - Anonymous

"It's crucial to understand the choreography on and off stage. From a dresser's point of view, the entire crew has their show choreographed, too. Be polite and listen to what your dresser tells you. They might have some insight into things you didn't even imagine. Stay calm and focused during the quick changes. Trust that no one will let you go on stage late or looking bad. Let the crew do their work, too. Don't run off in a panic. Say thank you at the end of the night, because everyone is in it together." - Franklin Hollenbeck (*Dresser of over 20 Broadway shows including: Newsies, Hair, Memphis, Tarzan, La Cage aux Folles, Suessical, Beauty and the Beast*)

"I love the swings who trust me. Dressers have valuable knowledge of each track that can help you, so it's important to listen and do what they tell you instead of fighting them." - Fran Curry (*Dresser: Bridges of Madison County, Nice Work if You Can Get It, Mary Poppins, Spamalot, Mamma Mia, Fosse, Titanic, The Music Man*)

"The fresh energy that a swing can bring to the cast is often magical and so needed. It's a constant reminder that the show is a living and breathing thing. I cherished the memories and images of entire casts piled 'head upon head' in the wings in support of the 'new guy'." - Tracy Terstriep Herber (*The Producers, Fosse, Will Rogers Follies, A Christmas Carol*)

"Most actors onstage were nice to me over the course of my career. The ones who weren't nice, were the ones I never expected. I realized that when other actors were being unkind to me, it was clearly about their own relationship to 'change'. Some people just can't handle it and it's more of a reflection about them than it is about you being a perfect swing." - Lisa Gajda (*Chaplin, Catch Me If You Can, Finian's Rainbow, Pal Joey, Cry Baby, The Times are A-Changin', Spamalot, Urban Cowboy, Movin' out, Kiss Me Kate, Sweet Smell of Success, Fosse, How To Succeed In Business Without Really Trying*)

"If you haven't been a swing before, it's like being forced to go back to University after ten years. Organization (Lord, what would I do without my index cards), flexibility to drop everything and run (with the exception of your index cards) and a positive attitude that you can do anything (with the help of your index cards). And most importantly, knowing that there will come a time, when you don't need your index cards" - Mary McCandless (*Showboat, Ragtime, Hairspray: The Movie*)

"Stay ahead of the game, especially in a new production! Even though the changes are happening daily, you must learn them and write everything down. You never know who may get sick during rehearsals, tech or previews! Don't wait to learn your parts until the show is frozen. It will be too late." - Jeanine Meyers *(Saturday Night Fever, Footloose)*

"When I was a swing, I would go into everyones' dressing rooms and say, 'If I'm in your way tonight, I promise I won't be the next time!'" - Dennis Stowe *(Aladdin, Annie, Leap of Faith, Shrek, The Apple Tree, Best Little Whorehouse in Texas, Dirty Rotten Scoundrels, A Little Princess, Wonderful Town, Man of La Mancha, Dreamgirls)*

"To be the best swing I can be is to realize that I am servicing a show the best way I can. It's my colleagues knowing they can count on me. It's the only time when 'being shot out of the cannon' actually means 'remain focused'. So satisfying." - Tug Watson *(National Tours: Evita, Young Frankenstein)*

"I found it was not about being perfect. It's about being 'practically perfect'...as Mary Poppins would say...and the ability to be able to shake it off when mistakes happen. It can sometimes feel like such a thankless job, yet so rewarding at the same time." - Mindy Franzese Catron *(Ragtime, Chitty Chitty Bang Bang, Joseph and the Amazing Technicolor Dreamcoat)*

"I think swings are the bravest people. They make bold choices in a split second in any given moment that further tell the story. They do this in their own way while staying true to the overall meaning and picture of the show. They are truly the heros of the show as they can be called upon at any given moment to assure the show continues. 'The show must go on.'" - Larry A Lozier JR *(National Tour of Cats)*

"Chet Walker passed on some personal advice to me in Fosse. He said, 'If, at the end of the night, you haven't killed anyone or yourself, you can walk out the stage door feeling so satisfied knowing you did that; you rose to the occasion. You should feel so damned proud of yourself for helping the show to go on'. Every time I was feeling low, I would hang on to that." - Deb Leamy *(Fosse, Never Gonna Dance, Sweet Smell of Success)*

"I loved being a swing! It made the show that much more exciting and spontaneous and intense. It meant 100% commitment and focus. It's about being ready and embracing the unexpected. Stay open and positive about not everything going perfectly." - Alice Rietveld (*The Music Man, Bells are Ringing, Aida, Annie Get Your Gun, Ragtime, West Side Story*)

"It was my favorite job of all. I was never bored, always on my toes, and everyone gave me accolades every time I went on. I started seeking out swing jobs because I enjoyed them more than regular ensemble tracks." - Regina Ahlgren (*Ragtime, Saturday Night Fever, Joseph and the Amazing Technicolor Dreamcoat, 42nd Street*)

"*I was swinging THE MUSIC MAN. The understudy was on for one of the leads, and I was on for her. The 'pick-a-little' ladies' scene is a famous, fast-paced patter scene and song. The understudy was dropping her lines and throwing off everyone. It was my job to start the next song by signaling the conductor with a head nod. In the midst of all the confusion of dropped lines, I just panicked and started the song without even looking at the conductor. All I heard was 'boom-chuck, boom-chuck' from the drummer as the conductor tried to catch the orchestra up to me.*" - Cynthia Leigh Heim

"*I went into a show as a replacement and was so happy. I just wanted to let my partners know that they could come to me with anything they wanted to work on. The usual protocol is to go through the dance captain to get help with partnering, but I was eager to please my partners. One partner in particular, started coming to me everyday with something for me to work on. She ended up getting so freaked out at the smallest things, that I had an extra half an hour rehearsal after my put-in to work with just her. She ended up making me feel insecure and the truth was, she really didn't even need me for some of the partnering stuff. She was a strong partner and was nit-picking every detail. I tried really hard to treat her as 'the person' versus 'the dance partner'. One day she gave me a note! Don't let those type of personalities allow you to question your abilities. It's most often about them and how they handle change versus your abilities. Yes, it will be different with each person, and hopefully, they can learn something from you, too, when you go on.*" - Anonymous

CHAPTER 16

Glossary of Theatre Terminology

10-out-of 12: There are certain rehearsal days allowed in the production contract called "10-out-of-12". This means there may be 10 hours of rehearsal allowed in a 12 hour span of a day without additional overtime paid. This can happen prior to the first public performance of a show.

A

AEA: (Actors' Equity Association) The association that represents professional stage actors and stage managers in live, scripted theatre. It regulates minimum salaries and working conditions.

AGMA: (The American Guild of Musical Artists). AGMA represents singers, dancers and other performers in operas and other classical music productions and concerts.

AGVA: (The American Guild of Variety Artists). AGVA represents performers in some Las Vegas showrooms, Radio City, some cabarets, comedy showcases, dance revues, circus and magic shows.

AS CAST: It is a term used when an actor has been hired for a job but the actual role they've been assigned may have parts yet to be determined. The creative team can decide how they want to use you in the show as they rehearse and create the show. Example: You may be asked to be the Doctor, Waiter or Mother in a scene that is not specified in your contract.

Assistant: This person helps a particular job title do its function. (Example: Assistant Director, Assistant Stage Manager, Assistant Choreographer, Assistant Lighting Designer)

Associate: This person is directly below, or next in line to a particular job title and helps them do his/her function. This position is higher in rank than an assistant. (Ex: Associate Director, Associate Choreographer, Associate Lighting Designer)

B

Backstage: The area behind the set, which is not seen by the audience.
Back Stage: A weekly entertainment trade publication that profiles the industry through articles, reviews and casting notices for theatre, film and television.

BC/EFA: Broadway Cares/Equity Fights AIDS is the Nation's leading industry-based, not-for-profit AIDS fund-raising and grant making organization.

Blend/Blending: This is a term used when more than one voice is singing. To have a nice blend is when all vocal parts are equal in volume and nothing in particular stands out from the rest.

Bobby Pins: A hair pin made of metal used to hold the hair or the "wig prep" in place. It is a double-pronged hair clip with one side straight and the other wavy for grip. They come in a variety of colors to match hair colors.

Breakdown: This refers to the casting notice that goes out to the entertainment community, listing the specific requirements for roles in a show. It can specify what they are looking for regarding principals and chorus.

Broadway: (the street) A boulevard running through the theatre district in New York City.

Broadway: (theatre) Any show performed in one of the 40 professional theatres, with 500 or more seats, located in the Theatre District and Lincoln Center along Broadway, in the borough of Manhattan, NY.

Broadway Box: Another term for the Theatre District in Manhattan. It primarily runs from 40th to 54th street, between 6th and 8th Avenue.

B-Roll: Supplemental video footage of the show that is intercut with main footage or interviews for promotional purposes.

Brush-Up Rehearsal: A rehearsal that occurs during the run of the show. The main focus is to perfect certain choreography, vocals and staging.

Business Rep: This is a business representative on staff at Actors' Equity, to be the liaison to the Broadway show and address any issues or concerns of the actors and management.

Buy-Out: An employer may "buy out" an employee's contract by making a single prepayment, so as to have no ongoing obligation to employ the person. Provisions for buy-out vary by contract.

C

Callboard: A bulletin board backstage upon which important information is placed such as: rehearsals and performance schedules, union and theater announcements, and notices intended for the entire cast.

Calling Desk: This is the area where one stage manager will sit and "call" the show cues over a headset to the rest of the crew. It will have monitors, lighting and fly rail cue switches and a place for the stage manager's calling script. It will likely be close to the stage and have direct visual access to it.

Calling Script: The book full of cues the stage manager creates, to help him or her call the show over the headsets to the backstage crew.

Call Time: This is the time you are personally required to be present at the theatre or studio to start working. It is listed on the rehearsal schedule and posted on the callboard the day before.

Cast: All the acting members of the company (onstage and off). The company of Actors hired for a production.

Cast Recording/Cast Album: The audio recording made of a production and sold commercially.

Casting Director: The person(s) in charge of facilitating auditions where actors sing, dance and act for the opportunity of a job in a show. The casting director maintains files of actors who may be right for the show in the future.

Choreographer: The person who designs the dance sequences and the musical staging in a production.

Chorus: Someone who is part of the larger, supporting cast for the majority of the time in a play or musical. Also referred to as "ensemble".

Clean Track: A term used when doing a sound or voice recording. When you can record a song or measures of a song and have no interference or noises on the recording. (Papers shuffling, coughing, hearing the click track on the vocal track)

Click Track: This is a synchronization tool used in musicals. Sometimes there are pre-recordings done for a musical that have to be synced during a show to the live orchestra and live singers. The musical director will put on a pair of headphones while conducting and use the pre-established metronome on the pre-recording to conduct the live show. The sound engineer will blend the sound of the pre-recorded click track and the live sound.

Company Manager: Someone who works for the general manager in charge of many daily aspects of the company. This includes (but is not limited to) dealing with performer's contracts, coordinating travel and housing, paychecks, arranging company show ticket reservations, and acting as the liaison between Equity and the company.

Comps: Tickets provided to an individual with no charge.

Cover/Covering: Term used in reference to being responsible for knowing another person's track. You may be told "You will cover Henry" or "You cover the female dancers".

Chart: A piece of paper with the stage diagram on it and other useful information about the production.

Creatives: This is a term that lumps together the decision-makers of the show. It could include the director, choreographer, designers and any of their associates or assistants.

D

Dance Belt: This is an anatomically supportive undergarment worn by males while performing. It hugs the genitalia snugly in place against the lower abdominal area to prevent pain or injury while performing. Most dance belts are of thong design but there are some manufacturers that have full bottom versions.

Dance Captain: This is the actor/dancer selected to rehearse all replacements and understudies. He or she is responsible for ensuring that the dances run smoothly throughout the run of a production.

Dark House: This refers to a theatre not currently in use.

Dark Night: This refers to the night of the week in which there is no performance.

(The) Deck: Another term for the floor of the stage.

Deluge Curtain: This is a fire curtain or safety curtain for precaution used in large proscenium theatres. It is usually made of iron or heavy fiberglass and is located right behind the proscenium arch. In some older theatres it is water that is stored and poured down in heavy amounts. The purpose is to protect the audience if there was ever a fire to start onstage.

Deputy: The cast of each production must elect a deputy or deputies to serve as a liaison between Equity and the company, to ensure the upholding of union regulations.

Director: The person who gives the actors blocking during the rehearsal process, and who works with them on such things as interpretation.

Downstage: A direction term that is used. The direction of "downstage" is towards the audience when you are standing onstage. The term originated when stages were raked or sloped towards the audience and you literally had to walk down the stage.

Dresser: This person assists the actor in putting on and removing costumes pieces. Broadway has union dressers, and actors do not do up each other's zippers to be helpful. The costumes cost many thousands of dollars and dressers are more experienced with garments if something were to get caught or torn. Actors, who try to help, may inadvertently harm something, and therefore, should not interfere with the dresser's job.

Dress Rehearsal: Usually the last rehearsal before the play is to be performed before an audience. This rehearsal is usually done with full costume and technical effects being used, and the play is performed straight through without stopping.

Dressing Rooms: The place backstage where the actors apply make up and put on costumes. Usually there are many dressing rooms to accommodate different leading roles, secondary roles, female chorus, male chorus and juvenile actors.

Dues: The fee paid by members to enable their union to represent them in negotiations, grievances, work site issues and legislative priorities. Basic dues are paid twice a year. Working dues are a percentage of your salary and are paid on a weekly basis.

E

Ensemble: This is another term meaning chorus. It's a group of complementary actors who contribute to a single effect of supporting the story of the play or musical.

Extension: It is a dance term denoting movement of limb away from body. If someone has "good extension", it usually means they are flexible. It can also be used as a contractual term. In this case, it would mean moving the contract end date so it would be longer than originally intended.

Extra: A person hired to provide atmosphere and background only. An Extra may not be identified as a definite character, either singly or within a group and may not be required to change make-up. An Extra may, however, make a single costume change. An Extra may not be rehearsed more than two weeks before the first public performance, may not speak except in omnes, may not sing (except with the consent of Equity in relation to a particular play), dance, or understudy and may not tour except with a pre-Broadway tryout of eight weeks or less.

Extraordinary Risk: This is a contract rider that indicates you are doing something "riskier than normal" on stage. It puts a flag up for the Workman's Comp Insurance Company, to allow for supplemental Workman's Comp payments if an actor was to get injured while performing something that was deemed extraordinary risk.

F

Favored Nation: The wages and/or terms of one actor's contract cannot be less than that of other cast members. This is a contract rider.

Fight Captain: This is the actor designated to rehearse all fight sequences with the current cast, replacements, and understudies. This person, with the assistance of the stage manager, insures that the fight sequences are properly maintained throughout the run of the production.

Fly Rail: The system of steel rails, ropes and counterweights in a theatre. It is mounted close to the walls and ceiling. Everything from curtains, sets, and lights are hung on these rails. Sometimes the rails are also used for aerial stunts done by performers. The rails are lowered and raised throughout the show by automation or a crew person and a series of counter-weights.

Fourth Wall: A term used in theatre to represent the imaginary wall at the front of the stage separating the audience from the performers. To "break the fourth wall" means to address or speak directly to the audience.

Frozen: A term used in reference to the show. If a show is "frozen", there will be no more changes made to the show. This is usually done close to opening or before the critics come to see the show.

Full Out/Full Voice: A term used when performing or rehearsing choreography and songs. It is assumed you will perform any lifts and extensions at their fullest and you are dancing the moves as if you were performing for an audience. It also means you will sing as if you were performing for an audience.

G

General Manager: Works for the producer and runs the business of the production, such as: issuing checks, keeping records, booking rehearsal facilities, and dealing with all departments.

Ghost Light: This is the one light plugged in and left onstage when all other lights in the theatre have been shut off. There are many conflicting thoughts as to whether this originated out of superstition or function.

GMA: An acronym for the Good Morning America television show on the ABC network. Many shows perform on this show because of the viewership and it shoots right in Times Square.

Green Room: A room backstage where the actors can lounge or await their entrance cues to go onstage. It can be one of the few areas people can eat in as well, although not every theatre has one. Eating backstage in other areas of old theatres can encourage the migration of mice, cockroaches and rats.

Guest List: This is a list that is kept at the stage door for every performance, informing the doorman who to expect and who to let in the theatre. If you have a guest who wants to see you backstage after the show, you should write your guest's name on that list.

Gypsy: This is a term that refers to a chorus actor. The term "gypsy" came from the idea that chorus actors would perform in many different Broadway shows and go from show to show.

Gypsy Robe: A long-standing Equity chorus tradition. The chorus person with the most Broadway chorus contracts will be presented with the Gypsy Robe on opening night. More information may be found on the Actors' Equity website (http://www.actorsequity. org/AboutEquity/GypsyRobe/gypsyhistory.asp)

H

Half-Hour: At half-hour before curtain time, all actors in the production are to be in the theatre. It is extremely important that all actors be backstage by this time to make sure everyone is accounted for and the production can start on time. There will be a "half hour" call made by stage management over the backstage speakers and they will check the callboard to make sure every actor has signed in by that time.

House: A term that refers to the seats in the theater where the audience sits. You will hear phrases like "Come and sit in the house" or "No food or drink in the house".

House Board: A board upon which the names of the cast may be displayed. This board is either located in the front of the theatre or in the lobby.

House Left: A directional term used. The direction of house left is "to your left" when you are in the audience and looking to the stage.

House Lights: The lights that illuminate the audience section of the theatre to aid them in getting to and from their seats. These lights go off during a show.

House Manager: The person who oversees the box office and ensures the seating and exiting of the audience. The theatre itself employs this person.

House Right: A directional term used. The direction of house right is "to your right" when you are in the audience and looking to the stage.

House Seats: These are considered the premium tickets or the best seats in the house. The theatre holds them for special purposes, and they won't be released to the public unless they know the seats won't be used. The cast may request and purchase these seats through the company manager. There are a finite number of these seats per show and the cost and availability differs with each production.

I

IATSE: (International Alliance of Theatrical Stage Employees). This is the union that represents the backstage crew.

Increment: A certain dollar amount that will be given to you above your contractual salary for additional duties assigned to you.

Initiation Fee: The initial amount it costs to join a union and become a member.

Intermission: The time between acts when the audience can get up to use the restroom, and the actors can rest or change into their next costume. Sometimes there are scenery changes that happen during this break in preparation for the next act.

J

Just Cause: Termination for a valid reason. The producer has the obligation to give the actor written notes of his/her failures and must give the actor the opportunity to correct them. If there is a dispute, the termination is subject to grievance (where applicable) and/ or arbitration.

L

Lav (Lavalier): This is a hands-free amplification system consisting of a small microphone and a transmitter that an actor will wear during a show. The mic can be concealed in the hair, below the wig, attached to glasses, hats or a piece of clothing. The transmitter would be worn either in the wig, or on the actor's body in a mic belt.

League of American Theatres and Producers (a.k.a. The League): A trade association that is made up of the producers on Broadway that collectively bargain the Production Contract with the performing unions.

Load In & Load Out: The first term refers to placing the set and equipment in the theatre and on the stage for a performance. The latter refers to removing the set and equipment from the theatre.

M

Mark/Marking: A term used when you physically/vocally move through the choreography/song but you don't perform the routine to its maximum amount. It is assumed you will not attempt the lifts or do anything that may put too much strain on your muscles or ligaments. This is used when the dancers' muscles have "cooled down" or when it is only necessary for blocking purposes to see where you need to be. It may be used as a "safety run" to give you some practise before trying it full out. When working with a partner, it's important to discuss what this term means to each other so one person doesn't attempt something and catch the other off-guard. It is also used for singers when the vocal chords are not warmed up or when the song is demanding on the voice and doing it repeatedly, at "full voice", may harm vocal chords. This term is also used for a specific place to be on the stage. For example, the director might say "Hit your marks" or "Be on your mark". This means that you have been given a specific place to be on the stage and that is your "mark".

Matinee: A performance given during the day.

Mic Belt: This is a pouch (attached to an elastic belt) that the actor wears to conceal the transmitter for a microphone. It can be worn on the waist, thigh, ribs, between the breasts, or anywhere that is comfortable.

Mic Tape: This is a special, clear adhesive tape used to attach the microphone chord to the actor's skin to prevent it from bulging out. It is commonly used on the back of the neck.

Mic-Up: A term used when the cast is asked to put microphones on for a rehearsal/show. The cast makes their way to the mic table, dressing room or other location to put on their mics. If you are not in costume, you may need to get a mic belt from wardrobe in order to hold the mic pack while rehearsing. There are also different options for attaching the mic in your hair, hat, or glasses. The sound department will discuss different ways with you to find the best option. There may be an elastic that goes around your head, or a hair/toupee clip that clips into your hair, or a bobby pin.

Musical Director: The person who teaches the actors their songs and sets the tempo of the delivery of songs. He/she usually conducts the orchestra and the actors during every performance.

N

National Tour: The title given to a touring production of a Broadway show.

Non-performing Actor: Someone who is not in the show every night, such as a swing, standby or a dance captain.

Notice: This is a piece of paper that management can put up on the callboard to announce the closing date of a production.

Number: This can be a measurement on the stage, such as stage left 5 or stage right 18. It can also be used to describe a scene from a musical, such as "Exit stage left when you finish the number". Number usually refers to a song and/or dance scene and not a book scene.

O

Off Broadway: Productions done in Manhattan, but away from the central theatre district, and refers to theatres with seating capacities of 499 or less. The categories of Off-Broadway theatres are determined by seating capacity.

Omnes: The whole cast; everyone; all.

Open Call: An audition held for a show in which anyone can attend. If the open call is an Equity call, then Equity performers are given preferential treatment and have regulations as to how the audition is run. If there is time and all of the Equity performers have been seen, the non-Equity performers may be seen.

Overtime: Work that extends beyond the contractually allowable hours and usually involves some additional payment.

P

Part: (Part vs Role) A part is a piece of a role. These two terms can mean different things depending on the contract.

Parts Determination: This is a list made when a representative of Actors' Equity comes to see the show and determines what "parts" of each actor's roles require certain recognition and payment, as well as determining "set move" payments, and extraordinary risk.

Per Diem: In addition to salary, the producer pays each actor a set amount for living expenses for each day the actor is away from home or on tour.

Performing Actor: Someone who is in the show every night.

Personal Leave: Excused days off for reasons important to the individual worker, such as getting married.

Pin Curls: This is a hairdressing technique used under wigs to secure the wigs to your own hair. If the hair was left straight, there is a chance the wigs could slip off. This is a technique to curl the hair and then fasten it to the scalp using bobby pins. This creates knobs or areas for pins to fasten the wig to the head.

Pink Contract: This refers to the color of the paper of the contract a chorus member signs. It's synonymous with a Chorus Contract.

(The) Pit: The area (often times below the stage) where the musicians sit and play during a show. There is a special area or podium where the conductor stands, in order to be seen by all the musicians and all of the actors onstage at the same time.

Place of Engagement: The city in which the show is performing.

Places: This is a term you will hear the stage manager call over the PA system and in the wings, when it is time to start the show. All actors are called to the stage area to take their positions for the top of the show.

Playbill or Program: The program the audience receives which contains the actors bios, pictures, as well as the names of the production team.

Players Guide: A directory of actors utilized by casting directors, producers, etc. It includes the actors' picture, credits, union affiliation and representation.

Point of Organization: The city designated as the home base for a tour. It is limited to either New York, Chicago, Los Angeles or San Francisco. If you are performing outside of the "point of organization", then you are entitled to per diem.

Press Agent: The person hired by management to advertise a production through setting up interview sessions, photo shoots, etc. This person or agency is hired to create excitement and interest in seeing the show for audiences so they buy tickets.

Pre-Production: The period of time during which work is done on a show prior to the first rehearsal.

Preview: Performances done for an audience prior to the official opening of the show, or before critics review a show. Changes in the play may occur during this period.

Principal: A category of employment in an Equity contract. The other two are chorus and stage manager.

Producer(s): This is a person or group of people who put together a production team and the financial backers; they generally oversee the business associated with mounting a show.

Production Contract: The contract for actors administered by Actors' Equity Association used for most Broadway shows and some National tours.

Prompt Book: The stage manager's book in which the blocking and technical cues are written. It is also referred to as a calling script.

Props: There are three distinct types of props; (a) hand held props actors either bring on stage with them or handle while on stage; (b) set or scenic props that are large and placed on stage before the beginning of the play or scene by the crew: (c) dress props are items placed on stage to give the illusion of reality.

Proscenium: This is the area of the theatre surrounding the opening of the stage, located in front of the scenery. This creates a "window" for the audience so the performers don't have to move around the stage to give a good view from all sides.

Put-In: A rehearsal conducted for a show already in production, to incorporate a new cast member, swing or understudy. The new actor goes through the entire role, sometimes in costume, with all the cast members (not in costume) and all of the technical elements that affect the new actor's track.

Q

Quick change: This is when an actor has a short amount of time to change costumes, wigs, and/or shoes. Usually the actor is assisted by a dresser to help facilitate the change. The time can range from a few seconds to about 30 seconds for a full costume, wig and shoe change.

Quick Rigged: This is when articles of clothing or shoes are altered to help facilitate a quick change. Shoes that used to have buckles may be changed to a hook or elastic. Shirts that look like they have buttons may have velcro hidden instead. Skirts and pants may have snaps or velcro instead of buttons and hooks.

R

Raked Stage: A stage that is slanted downwards toward the audience.

Retroactive Pay: Wages due for past services, frequently required when wage increases are made effective as of an earlier date, or when contract negotiations are extended beyond the expiration date of the previous agreement, or when parts determinations are made.

Rider: Special contract provisions are called riders. They generally immediately follow the face of the contract.

Role: (Role vs Part) A sum of all the "parts" an actor plays. These terms can mean different things, depending on the contract.

Resident Director/Choreographer: A person who is contracted to maintain the show after the director and choreographer leave. They would usually take care of teaching direction and/or choreography instead of the stage managers and/or dance captains. Not every show hires this position.

Ross Reports: This is an entertainment resource book that is published monthly in New York and it contains a detailed listing of talent agents, casting directors, commercial producers and advertising agencies. This publication is primarily geared toward film and television.

Rule book: Each of the contracts that Actors' Equity Association administers has a rule book, which lists all of the terms and conditions allowable under a specific contract.

Run-of-the-Play: The dates that a show is open, which is dictated by ticket sales. The closing of the show is not a date known or specified; it is something that will be determined as the show sells.

S

SAG-AFTRA (Screen Actors Guild -American Federation of Television and Radio Artists): The union that represents actors, dancers, announcers, DJ's, puppeteers, program hosts, news writers, news directors, stunt performers, broadcast journalists, recording artists, voice-over artists, and other media professionals in radio, TV, Film, internet and other media.

Scale: Minimum salary for services under a union contract. This amount is dictated by the union and can change from contract to contract and year to year.

Scene: A unit of dialogue in a play or musical that portrays a certain situation. Plays and musicals are made up of many scenes.

SDC (Stage Directors and Choreographers Society): This is the union that represents Broadway directors and choreographers.

Secret vote/secret ballot: When you individually write your decision down on a piece of paper and it is counted anonymously. This is usually done at a meeting called by the Equity deputy where the assembled cast votes on a production related matter.

Set Designer: The person responsible for designing and overseeing the construction of a stage set.

Sexual Harassment: Any unwarranted or repeated sexual comments, looks, suggestions or physical contact that creates an uncomfortable working environment.

Show Bible: A term used for the collection of information pertaining to that show. Also referred to as "The Bible".

Show Curtain: The large curtain, usually heavy fabric, that rises at the beginning of a show to let the audience know the play or musical has started. The show curtain will rise at the beginning of each act and lower to the stage at the end of each act.

Sign-in (sheet): By "half hour", all the actors must sign in on a sheet posted on the callboard. All the actors' names will be typed out, and the actor has to initial beside his/her name when they enter the building. Once you sign in, you must remain in the building so that stage management can reach you over the PA system.

Sitzprobe: A seated rehearsal where singers sing with the orchestra, focusing integration of the two groups. It is often the first rehearsal where the orchestra and singers rehearse together. The musical director will run the rehearsal and no blocking or movement is done.

Specialty: This is when a chorus person is asked to do a featured dance, vocal or acting bit within a play/musical that makes them stand out from the rest of the chorus. It's usually something that propels the story forward and is recognizable to the audience.

Split-track: When someone has to perform more than one track during a show. This occurs when more than one actor is out and the most important parts of each of their tracks get combined and performed by one person.

Spot Lights: These are the bright lights that are usually controlled by technicians during the show. The purpose is to have a brighter light on someone or something, to draw the audience's attention.

Stage Door: This is the actors' and employees' entrance to the theatre. A person or video camera guards it. This is where you enter and exit the theatre daily.

Stage Doorman: The person who guards the stage door and who knows the reason everyone comes in and out of the theatre. He/she is there for security reasons.

Stage Left: A directional term that is used. The direction of stage left is "to your left" when you are onstage and looking out into the audience.

Stage Manager(s): Someone who maintains the prompt book/calling script and is hired to call the show. There will be one head stage manager and many assistants to help. They will organize the daily schedules, help run rehearsals, teach staging, manage props personnel, and oversee set moves and scenery. They also uphold the union rules and rights by keeping track of rehearsal hours, break times, etc.

Stage Right: A directional term that is used. The direction of stage right is "to your right" when you are onstage and looking out into the audience.

Stand-by: Someone who learns the track of a principal role but is not part of the performing cast. This person is usually hired specifically to cover a principal role that is one of the main leads. Some productions will ask the stand by to stay backstage during a show and others will have him/her be within close proximity to the theatre and be reachable in a moment's notice.

Step Outs: This is an older term not often used anymore. It means the same as a "specialty". It's when a member of the chorus has a vocal, dance or acting feature.

Supplemental Workers Compensation: Coverage that supplements workers' compensation/disability benefits. The state administers a certain amount of funds when an actor is injured on the job. This supplemental insurance can help pay more to bridge the gap between what the state pays and what the actor would be paid if he/she were still in the show receiving their full salary.

Swing (full): A non-performing member of the chorus who learns the tracks of the performing members of the chorus and performs them when said chorus is not able to perform his/her own track.

Swing (partial): A person in the performing chorus who learns the tracks of the other performing chorus members for specific "numbers" or scenes. For example: if someone got hurt during the scene before, the partial swing would already be in wig and costume and be able to step into any chorus track for the next number.

Swing (vacation): A Person who is hired when an actor is out of the show for any number of reasons (vacation, injury, personal days). This person is hired on an "as-needed" basis. They are not full time and may be asked to work in different companies of the same show, such as Broadway, National Tours or International productions.

Swing (universal): A person who is hired by a producer when there are multiple companies of the same show. They are hired full time and would go from company to company if the shows were on tour and/or on Broadway. They can be asked to go wherever needed, which could take them out of New York City, the State, or the Country.

Swing Out: When a swing is put onstage for a show to cover a chorus track while that chorus person sits in the house to watch the show. Some shows do "swing outs" for each cast person to get a chance to see the show. Some shows do regular swing outs to help the chorus' bodies get a little rest and hopefully help with the physical health of the company. Some shows do not do swing outs because the creative team prefers to have the original cast onstage and minimize variables unless absolutely necessary.

T

Table Read: When the company sits around a table to read (and possibly sing) through the entire play or musical. The purpose is for everyone in the room to hear the entire show in order to understand it better, without having to stand up and perform it on a stage or in a rehearsal room. This is often done in the beginning of a rehearsal process.

Tannoy: This is a term used for the public-address system in a theatre in which you can hear the stage manager's calls and announcements. Each dressing room usually has its own speaker with a volume control.

Term Contract: This is a contract with specified employment lengths. It can be a term where the producer asks the performer to stay for a certain amount of time within the run-of-the-play in exchange for extra payment. It could be a term where the producer and actor have a contract until a certain date, at which time it may or may not be renewed.

Title Page: The page of a PLAYBILL that lists information about the production.

TKTS: This is a ticket booth in Times Square operated by the Theatre Development Fund which sells discounted theatre tickets on the day of the show.

TONYS: The awards granted by the American Theatre Wing and the Broadway League. The proper name is the Antoinette Perry Awards, for outstanding excellence in theatre. It is named after Antoinette Perry, a legend in American theatre and cofounder of the American Theater Wing. The first award was given in 1947.

Toupet Clips (wig clips): These are clips that are used to fasten the mic chords to an actor's hair. They come in multiple colors to match the color of the hair/wig.

Track: Refers to the collective performance aspects of one chorus person. A swing may be required to learn multiple tracks.

Trail: This is a term used when one actor wants to follow another actor backstage throughout the course of a show. It's referred to as "trailing an actor". It is used when understudies or swings want to see the entrances, exits, prop, sound, wig and costume change details of an actor they are responsible for covering.

Tryout: This term is often used for "out-of-town tryouts", when a Broadway show goes out of town to mount the show first. This allows for changes to be made away from the Broadway critics before coming to Broadway with a show.

Turnaround: The number of hours between the end of work on one day and the beginning of work on the next day.

Tutor: The person hired to teach school-aged children. This person is often used during the rehearsal period when the children have to be accessible by the production and yet put in a certain number of school hours.

U

Underdress: This is when an actor puts on multiple layers of costumes to assist in a quicker costume change. An entire new costume or part of a costume can be worn under the current one onstage.

Understudy: A member of the chorus who learns the track of a principal role and who is prepared to perform the role, should the actor portraying the role be unable to perform.

Unemployment Insurance: Monetary contributions are made by the employer on the employee's behalf to the state fund. Should the employee be dismissed or the show close, they may receive unemployment benefits for a specific period of time.

Upstage: A directional term that is used. The direction of "upstage" is away from the audience when you are standing onstage. The term originated when stages were raked or sloped towards the audience and you literally had to walk up the stage.

V

Valuables: There may be a "valuables" collection done before the show by stage management. Any actor can turn in wallets, rings, watches, or anything of value (within limits) to be locked away in a safe place during the show to avoid theft.

W

White Contract: Term used to refer to the color of the paper signed by an actor doing principal work.

Wig Cap: This is a nylon cap that is placed over a "prepped head" (pin curled or wrapped). It secures the wig prep in place and helps secure the pins used to attach the wig to the actor's head.

Wig Glue: An adhesive used to attach the lace of a wig onto the actor's skin. This helps hold the wig lace in place and prevents the lace from sticking out. It is removed by rubbing a cotton ball soaked in adhesive remover over the glued area. Wig glue is always put on by hair department personnel and not the individual actor.

Wig Prep: A technique used to prepare the actor's hair for securing a wig. It can be done with pin curls and/or a combination of wrapping the hair.

Work Rules: Rules regulating on-the-job standards and conditions of work in the collective bargaining agreement. Work rules are negotiated between the union and management.

Work Week: The Equity work week runs from Monday to Sunday, with Thursday being the pay day.

Workers' Compensation Insurance: Insurance supplied by the producer to cover medical expenses that result from an on-the-job injury.

Wrangler: The person hired by the producer to be the guardian of the juvenile actors during the performance. Parents of juvenile actors are not allowed to be backstage after half hour or during a show.

Index